To FRUIT STREET AND BEYOND

The Massachusetts General Hospital Surgical Residency

DR. FREDRIC JARRETT

Archway Publishing books may be ordered through booksellers or by contacting:

Archway Publishing
1663 Liberty Drive
Bloomington, IN 47403
www.archwaypublishing.com
1 (888) 242-5904

Because of the dynamic nature of the Internet, any web addresses or links contained in this book may have changed since publication and may no longer be valid. The views expressed in this work are solely those of the author and do not necessarily reflect the views of the publisher, and the publisher hereby disclaims any responsibility for them.

Any people depicted in stock imagery provided by Thinkstock are models, and such images are being used for illustrative purposes only. Certain stock imagery © Thinkstock.

ISBN: 978-1-4808-3325-8 (sc)
ISBN: 978-1-4808-3326-5 (hc)
ISBN: 978-1-4808-3327-2 (e)

Library of Congress Control Number: 2016910886

Print information available on the last page.

Archway Publishing rev. date: 09/13/2016

CONTENTS

Introduction vii

Chapter 1:   Intern Exams.. 1

Chapter 2:   Rules of Engagement and the MGH Lexicon 8

Chapter 3:   Internship 13

Chapter 4:   More Internship 32

Chapter 5:   Private Service 40

Chapter 6:   Emergency Ward.. 52

Chapter 7:   Ward Service 63

Chapter 8:   Vascular 73

Chapter 9:   Cardiac.. 85

Chapter 10: Hiatus.. 93

Chapter 11: Then And Now.. 106

Chapter 12 118

Bibliography/Acknowledgements 123

INTRODUCTION

This book is not an autobiography. It is a book that needed to be written because our group of interns and residents trained at the end of an era, now long passed, when general surgery was predominant and all-inclusive. I am merely the conduit of these recollections.

General surgery at the time of my internship and junior residency encompassed general surgery as we now know it, plus cardiothoracic and vascular surgery, plastic surgery and burns, transplant surgery, and critical care medicine. We did the bulk of the head and neck tumor surgery, despite competition from our neighbor, the Massachusetts Eye and Ear Infirmary.

At the time, it was possible to take the examination for board certification in thoracic surgery without a formal residency if one had performed a sufficient number of cardiac and thoracic operations. Most of the chief residents did so. Although we had fully trained surgeons in teaching roles in all aspects of surgery, the absence of subspecialty training programs meant that the general surgery residents were the junior and senior house-officers in these areas, as well as in gynecology.

All of the senior faculty had trained at the Massachusetts General Hospital and many had taken more specialized training elsewhere and then returned. Not once during my training did I hear any of them discuss remuneration or economics. They were available for consultative advice or to assist in the operating room, but the patients we cared for were admitted to the resident-run service, then called the ward service, and we assumed full responsibility for their care. We were almost completely autonomous.

About the middle of my residency, changes began to appear. Additional training leading to board certification was offered in cardiothoracic and plastic surgery, and eventually a fellowship was established in vascular surgery as well. The first residents in the subspecialty areas were chosen from our own program, as the Mass General wanted to be sure of the product that would emerge.

A gynecology residency was begun. A separate department of emergency medicine was established, whose residents shared responsibility with us in the emergency ward. After training, our alumni excelled in their communities and in academics. Our residency did not have an obligatory one or two years in the research laboratories, and the department of surgery was as proud of the residents who entered private practice as it was of those of us who followed an academic career.

The description of the residency experience is based on my recollections supplemented by those of my friends and colleagues.

CHAPTER 1:   INTERN EXAMS

Always read the X-rays carefully.

When I sat on a hard wooden bench outside the chairman's office at the Mass General, waiting to be grilled by the so-called "final committee," I felt reasonably comfortable taking oral examinations. But like all applicants, I was intimidated.

I did not realize that the same procedure for selecting interns had been in place since at least the 1890s.

Director Emeritus Dr. Frederic Washburn's *The Massachusetts General Hospital, Its Development 1900–1935,* told that "candidates waited and shivered and trembled on benches in the corridor to the westward of the library. One at a time they were ushered in by the Director to sit at one side of the long table, the other three sides of which were occupied by Visiting Surgeons—a very trying ordeal for a young medical student. When the quiz was completed the student would be allowed to retire through the easterly door, to return to his room, usually in the south end of Boston, there to await the decision as to his fate."

As I recall, only the MGH and the Peter Bent Brigham had an oral examination for prospective interns, held on one day only, where all the senior surgeons cancelled elective surgery to form a hierarchy of committees. All the other hospitals I applied to simply had two or three surgeons interview the applicant instead.

The MGH (which Harvard students said stood for Man's Greatest Hospital) was the most sought-after surgical training program at Harvard, followed by the Peter Bent Brigham and Boston City. The chairmen at the latter two as well as the Lahey Clinic, Johns Hopkins Hospital, and Yale were alumni of the MGH training program.

The MGH's formidable list of milestones included the first public demonstration of ether anesthesia in 1846, the first description of the pathology of appendicitis by MGH pathologist Reginald Fitz, the first social service department, the first morbidity and mortality (M & M) conferences, and promulgation of outcomes research by E. Amory Codman in the early 1900s. MGH surgeons were responsible for early contributions to thyroid and parathyroid surgery by Olive Cope, pericardiectomy for constrictive pericarditis by Edward Churchill, the first clinical description of a herniated lumbar disk in the 1930s, seminal contributions to burn therapy after the Coconut Grove fire in 1942, and the first successful human limb reimplantation by Ronald Malt in 1962.

The MGH provided roughly half of hospital teaching for Harvard medical students. The weekly Clinicopathologic Conferences (CPC's) published in *The New England Journal of Medicine* were used and puzzled over by medical students and faculty alike. They, and the MGH, also had a worldwide audience thanks to the State Department, which provided copies to 160 medical schools abroad, along with lantern slides.

*The Bulfinch Building, named a national
historic monument in 1970 (Courtesy of the
Massachusetts General Hospital)*

The MGH was a rectangular training program, meaning that all the interns selected could complete the five years required to take general surgery boards. The department of surgery could offer this guarantee because a number of people would do two or three years of general surgery residency and then enter a subspecialty residency in orthopedics, neurosurgery, or urology. In contrast, pyramidal programs, where only one or two residents finished the program or became "super-chiefs," were forced to let capable residents go after two or three years or ask them to spend several years in the research lab.

The MGH was the first-choice internship for fourth-year Harvard students going into surgery and, we were told, for the other U.S. medical schools as well. There were nine clerks for the U.S.

Supreme Court justices, thirty-six Rhodes scholars for North America, nineteen White House fellows, and twelve surgical intern positions at the MGH. Approximately half of the interns were chosen from Harvard, which made the odds slightly better, but nevertheless daunting. Each year, the first twelve applicants listed by the MGH in the matching program were the twelve selected, as they had all listed the MGH as their first choice.

I had done well in medical school but was not at the top of my class and had not been elected to AOA, the medical honor fraternity. Such election was very difficult for a transfer student, and I had transferred into the third year at Harvard after two years at Dartmouth Medical School, which was then a two-year school. I felt that many of my classmates seeking a surgical internship had better academic records than I.

I did not think I would be selected for the MGH internship. I thought that I had a better chance at the Peter Bent Brigham, where I'd had my third-year surgery and medicine clerkships and had worked in the research lab for two summers getting to know some of the surgical faculty. I had already been through the examination at the Peter Bent Brigham and proceeded easily to the MGH senior committee.

Facing oral examiners who were in the Harvard pantheon of preeminent surgeons, was stressful for any medical student. Sitting at the end of a table facing senior faculty, many of whom had written the chapters in our surgical textbooks, made it difficult to be self-confident.

Another applicant waiting with me related that a previous examinee, an All-American football player who was second in his class in a southern medical school, had left the room in tears.

The entire internship examination process was business-like and foreboding. Many applicants came from a great distance, some as far as the west coast. If they did not pass the first and second committees, they were given a smile and a handshake by the department secretary along with a meal ticket for lunch in the hospital cafeteria.

We all eventually realized that the purpose of the examination was not only to test our knowledge base, but to see how we behaved under stress, gauge our self-confidence, observe our body language, and see whether we would admit to not knowing an answer or try to fake through a difficult question. If you obviously knew the correct answer, the examiners would cut you off and proceed to the next question. Obvious strategy: Don't answer too quickly.

Another potential trap was a question requiring the reading of an X-ray. One candidate was shown a chest X-ray and told it was of a male with a lung mass; he was able to correctly point out breast shadows on the film, demonstrating that the patient was a female. Lesson learned: Never trust someone else's reading of an X-ray on your patient. Do something yourself to be sure it's done correctly.

My own first committee examination was relatively benign. I was asked about indications for operation on aortic aneurysms, calcium metabolism, the blood supply to the thyroid gland, calcium replacement and pancreatitis, treatment of emergency chest injuries, and several questions about types of hiatus hernias.

Surgical history, literature, and musical trivia were fair game.

"Can you name the surgeons who have won the Nobel Prize in Medicine?"

"Define *death*."

"What will be the treatment of breast cancer thirty years from now?"

Another frequent question was to ask the candidate to identify the four men from Johns Hopkins in John Singer Sargent's portrait *The Four Doctors*. This question was deemed too easy for the applicants from Johns Hopkins, so it was given to the Harvard applicants. Everyone else except the Harvard applicants was shown a picture of the first demonstration of ether at the MGH.

An outstanding resident a few years ahead of me, who had been first in his class at Baylor, was asked to discuss Buerger's disease and provided an erudite discussion. On the way home, he was told that the vascular surgeon who had asked the question did not think Buerger's disease was a real entity.

The "final committee" consisted of Dr. Paul S. Russell, the department chairman, and nine other senior individuals, several of whom were subspecialty division chairmen who had authored chapters in the textbooks we used. I was asked about wound debridement, delayed primary wound closure, trophic ulcers, Dupuytren's contracture, and a number of extensive questions on hemopneumothorax illustrated by an X-ray of a young man with a collapsed lung and a fluid level at the lung base.

I thought I handled these questions well, and then at the end of the final question, one of the examiners asked, "Jarrett, is there anything else you would like to point out on this X-ray?"

At last. My chance to go to the head of the class.

"Yes, sir," I replied. "You told me this patient is a thirty-year-old male and he has calcification of his costal cartilages. This indicates that the patient's ancestors are either from Portugal or Ireland, since no other ethnic groups have premature calcification of the costal cartilages."

I had been told this "pearl" by a radiology professor during an elective. It has long since been disproven. My answer was followed by snicker from all present. I wondered if they were speculating as to whether I was the smartest medical student they had ever seen or whether they should get me out of the room before the laughter was uncontrollable.

I felt I had done well when they asked me a couple of final softball questions about Professor Rene Leriche, a preeminent French surgeon whose biography I had published after spending a summer in France between my second and third years in medical school, thanks to a generous student grant.

When I eventually finished training, went through the rites of passage, and faced the oral examinations for American and Canadian boards in general and vascular surgery, I found them much easier than the MGH intern examinations I took as a fourth-year medical student.

After completing training and interviewing residency applicants in Wisconsin and Pittsburgh, I realized the importance of being able to take measure of an applicant's logic and thought processes and to see how he handles himself under the stress of an oral examination (less stress than an emergency operation in the middle of the night on a complicated patient with unfamiliar assistants). I realized that oral examiners are consciously or unconsciously asking themselves, "Do I want this person to be called to see my patient for an emergency at one in the morning?"

CHAPTER 2: RULES OF ENGAGEMENT AND THE MGH LEXICON

"We come from a world where we have known incredible standards of excellence, and we dimly remember beauties which we have not seized again."

—Thornton Wilder,
The Bridge of San Luis Rey

The MGH was very informal about most things. There were few rules and regulations but many traditions, which were passed on from house officer to house officer.

We had no contract. Our one-page letter of reappointment came each year, stating that the trustees had VOTED (always in capital letters) to recommend our appointment at the (given) level. Our salary was mentioned as was the fact that the hospital provided laundry and uniforms.

We had health insurance for ourselves and for our families, but there was never a health insurance card nor a named insurance company, co-pays, or deductibles. It was understood that we and our families had full health coverage with any hospital in Boston and full coverage for all prescription medications.

Uniforms were provided and consisted of a short white coat, white pants and a collarless white shirt with snap buttons, obviating the need for a necktie; these saved on laundry, dry cleaning, and new clothes. Senior residents were allowed to wear their own shirts and ties if they wished. Visiting surgeons wore suits or short white coats. No surgeon at the MGH wore a long white lab coat. Only surgeons were permitted to wear scrubs at the MGH, but never outside the operating room.

Parking was provided. One month annual vacation was allowed, but not during the internship year. Residents lobbied the program director to get a thirty-one-day month for their vacation.

At grand rounds, the senior visiting surgeons sat in the first row, followed by more junior visiting surgeons behind them, followed by the house staff behind them.

There was no mention of absences because of sickness, and there were no sick days. We were never sure whether we were not allowed to get sick or just did not dare to get sick. Almost everyone was on duty in the hospital every other night.

If you were sick and unable to work, the resident you alternated with might have to be in hospital for three or more consecutive nights. In emergencies, the resident on the endoscopy rotation, which had no night call, might be drafted. Or someone on vacation would be abruptly ordered back to work.

Mostly we followed the example of the attending surgeons and their work ethic. Dr. Wyland Leadbetter, a versatile technician who was chief of urology, was exemplary in his work habits and dedication to his patients. Usually, one general surgery resident each year chose to become a urologist after rotating on his service, including one of my roommates, Reid Pitts.

Dr. Leadbetter was from Maine and was succinct in his conversation. He started rounds every morning at 6 a.m. with his resident, often sitting on the edge of the bed, always letting the patient know he was concerned and empathetic. After operating all day, he walked home for dinner, then returned to the hospital in the evening to check on his patients.

When the resident went to see Dr. Leadbetter the morning after he had undergone a pulmonary resection, the nurse told him, "You'd better hurry up. He put on his bathrobe, picked up his chest tube and bottles, and went to make rounds on his patients."

One resident developed a kidney stone, which is extremely painful. Unwilling to take time off, he had us start an intravenous on him and ran in a large quantity of fluid and some intravenous Demerol until the stone was passed and he could remove the I.V.and return to work.

Another resident had a bad episode of flu while in the Emergency Ward and could hardly stand because of dehydration. The rest of the team put him into an empty bed and ran in two liters of IV fluid over a few hours, enabling him to return to work upright.

The Mass General also had a unique vocabulary, recognizable to the indoctrinated but unknown to the rest of the world. Medical students were *studs*. The intern was the *tern* or the *pup*. The esophagus was the *goose*. The umbilicus was the *gimp*. In the OR for a major procedure, we were told to prep the patient from *guzzle to zorch*. I think that meant from neck to pubis but was never sure.

A fourth-year medical student taking an elective in surgery was a *striker*. The senior resident appointed as chief resident for the following year was the *dauphin*. The emergency room senior resident, who triaged the patients entering, was the *gauleiter*, a distasteful term for anyone familiar with the history of World War II.

The senior resident on the private service was the *scoutmaster*. The monthly combined surgery grand rounds was the *Superbowl*. A newly minted surgeon employed for a year or two by one of the established practices was the *gnome*.

An appendiceal retractor was *grandfather's retractor*. Everyone called it that. George Richardson's grandfather, Maurice Howe Richardson, a legendary MGH chief of surgery, had designed it and claimed he could do an appendectomy with an incision no longer than the retractor's end. When I asked for grandfather's retractor at subsequent institutions, no one knew what I was talking about.

Patients did not die at the Mass General Hospital. They *went to Allen Street*. This street no longer exists. It ran behind the Bullfinch Building which was constructed in 1821. The hospital built a mortuary there in 1874 that faced houses and tenements across the street. The larger of its two doors could accommodate horse-drawn hearses. Allen Street is now that portion of Blossom Street lying between Emerson Place and the MGH's Gray

Building. Dr. Lewis Thomas wrote a longish poem about Allen Street in his book *The Youngest Science.*

There were no operative consent forms when I was a resident, nor for many years thereafter. The hospital assumed that if you were a patient at the MGH, you consented to the operation your surgeon proposed. Visiting surgeons never documented informed preop consent in the patient's chart, and they almost never wrote daily progress notes.

There was no procedure specific credentialing of the visiting surgeons. When the Joint Commission identified this as a deficiency during one of its periodic inspections, Dr. Austen was perplexed. Everyone was fully trained as a general surgeon, did what he was most expert at, and referred patients needing other procedures to the appropriate colleague. Why credential for specific procedures?

Mostly, we were able to dedicate our energies to taking care of patients, and learning.

CHAPTER 3:   INTERNSHIP

"Leave no 'tern unstoned"

—Anonymous MGH axiom

The chief resident briefed the new interns at the start of their rotation on one of the two ward services.

"If a patient is hypovolemic, we resuscitate with plasma or blood. Crystalloid solution is used across town, not here," he told us.

"If any patient pulls out a tube and has to go back to the OR, the intern will be on the train home the next day."

"This is how you flag a tube," he continued, applying benzoin and a large piece of adhesive tape to the patient's abdomen next to the exit site of the tube, then another piece of tape around the gastrostomy, creating two flanges, so that it could be immobilized with a safety pin to the underlying tape.

Protecting tubes and drains was a very serious part of postoperative care.

A significant part of our patient population entered with hemorrhage from the upper gastrointestinal tract, either from peptic ulcers or from esophageal varices caused by cirrhosis. The double jejunostomy tubes placed after gastric resection were marked "drain me" and "feed me" as excess gastric contents from the "drain me" tube could be instilled in the "feed me", preventing electrolyte losses. These were "flagged" to the skin.

Hence was the origin of the "pull me" tube. Patients with bleeding esophageal varices were a prohibitive risk for emergency operation, and we strove to control the bleeding with a Linton tube passed into the stomach through the nose or mouth. This device had large balloons which were inflated to tamponade the bleeding, and needed to be taped to a football helmet and placed on traction constructed at the foot of the patient's bed. These patients were alcoholics with a proclivity for pulling out any accessible tube, which could result in fatality in this setting. A common preventive measure was to allow a small tube to be taped to the helmet, and dangled so as to be visible to the patient. This we called the "pull me" tube and was intended to distract the patient's attention from the more crucial tube employed to arrest esophageal bleeding.

So began internship for twelve of us on July 1.

We were all certain that many of the applicants not chosen were more qualified than we were. We were aware that in the event of a sudden vacancy in the program, the MGH could telephone almost any resident in the United States and have him in Boston in twenty-four hours. We knew because they told us so.

The men one or two years ahead of us were confident, relaxed, self-assured. Would we be that poised one year from now?

What does it take to become a highly skilled surgeon? Malcolm Gladwell, in *Outliers,* talks about ten thousand hours needed to become an NHL star or a concert violinist. Working approximately 90–100 hours per week for five years, minus vacation time, meant we worked between twenty-two and twenty-four thousand hours during our training.

We realized that the habits we formed would follow us throughout our careers. If you make it through the MGH internship, you can do anything. Learn the right habits, and you will be a good surgeon forever.

Most of us had a surgical experience as medical students, limited to a few months on a surgical service with no real responsibility other than trying to maximize our learning. We couldn't sew or tie knots. We couldn't do the simplest part of an operation without a more senior resident directing every minor move. They joked about giving us surgical gloves with fingers at the end of the year.

The thought of being responsible for a service of fifteen to twenty patients seemed overwhelming. The nurses knew more about surgery than we did.

In contrast to current bureaucratic complexities, which grow each year, our orientation required only one day—the day before we were officially on the payroll—of filling out tax forms, being issued uniforms and a pager, being assigned to an on-call room, and sitting through a few short presentations on administrative issues.

The interns' on-call rooms were in the Parkman Building, which was physically separate from the remainder of the hospital. It was an old building that had been condemned but wouldn't be demolished until some years later. The steam heating was somewhat erratic, but satisfactory. There was no air conditioning. When called in the middle of the night, we needed to go outside and cross a courtyard to enter the hospital in the unpredictable Boston weather.

The rooms were generally doubles. There was adequate storage space for clean uniforms and toiletries. Civilian clothes were superfluous. We quickly learned to rearrange our room assignments *ad hoc* to create functionally single rooms so we wouldn't be awakened by the other intern's phone calls as well as our own.

Our college friends in other professions asked, "When do you get to go home when you're on duty?" We did not find the question amusing.

We were on duty in the hospital every other night and every other weekend. The middle level and senior residents had the same call schedule. Only the chief residents were allowed to take call from home, but in reality they were in the hospital as much or more than the other residents.

The two mirror-image ward services were designated east and west, named after the original services housed in the Bulfinch Building in the nineteenth century, when they had existed for the care of the indigent. The east service's chief had been Dr. Arthur W. Allen, and the west's chief Dr. Edward Delos "Pete" Churchill, who had been the army's surgical consultant in the North African and Mediterranean theater during World War II.

There was a long rivalry between the two services, and a lot of tradition. Photos of past chief residents, later illustrious surgeons, hung in the interns' call room next to the nurses' station, where we tried to get a few hour's interrupted sleep when on duty. When a nurse would wake us with a problem in the middle of the night, we were sure they were watching us to see how we would handle it.

Each service had its own floor in the White Building in a T-shaped configuration, with an east, west, and south wing, the last our *de facto* ICU for the most ill patients, particularly those requiring ventilators. The east and west wings were either all-male or all-female, and each had an intern, junior resident, and senior resident assigned.

The White Building, where east and west surgical services each had a floor for inpatients (Courtesy of the Massachusetts General Hospital)

Computers and fax machines did not exist yet. Each intern carried the "scut board" everywhere except in the operating room or shower. This was a clipboard listing patient names and their laboratory work, X-ray findings, and other pertinent information.

Each intern was totally responsible for knowing everything about his patients, which meant filling out laboratory, X-ray, and blood transfusion requisitions and becoming familiar with home situations that affected discharge planning. At the end of the day, lab results were retrieved, entered by hand onto the scut board, and ultimately incorporated into the daily progress notes that we wrote after making evening rounds.

Rounds began at 7:00 a.m. and were very formal, even military. We began in the emergency ward, where a three-person team attached to our service would present the newly admitted patients to the chief resident. There was an "overnight ward" where we could admit patients for up to seventy-two hours for workup and stabilization. After seventy-two hours, they would either be transferred to our main floor, moved to another service, or sent home.

On our floor, the intern or junior resident on duty the previous night would recite the daily catechism, "presenting" each patient to the senior or chief resident, summarizing the events of the prior twenty-four hours.

The intern or junior resident coming on duty would carry the order book and transcribe the orders dictated by the senior or chief resident for diet, intravenous fluids, laboratory work, patient activity, and necessary subspecialty consults.

"Mr. Donizetti is now two days after emergency gastrectomy for a bleeding duodenal ulcer and is hemodynamically stable with minimum nasogastric drainage, and began ambulation yesterday. He has a low-grade fever, probably due to bronchitis, and has been suctioned. CBC and electrolytes are normal. Can probably have the NG tube removed today and start on liquid diet tomorrow."

Sometimes you were up all night in the OR or with one or two ill patients and did not have all the information at hand. If the nurses liked you, they would help out by standing out of the chief resident's line of vision and signaling answers to us.

"How many units of blood did this patient need overnight?" Two fingers held up. Reputation saved.

Speaking out of turn was discouraged, unless you had a particularly cogent comment to make. The chief resident was the judge of your presentation and comments. Succinctness was a virtue. If you did not know the relevant and important information, you quickly learned to have it at hand. Without this organized structure, we would have never been able to finish morning rounds and get to the OR on time.

After rounds, those having scheduled operations would proceed to the operating room. The end of rounds was notoriously unpredictable because there was inevitably something that needed to be done: patients who were unstable and needed immediate attention, or emergency operations that had been scheduled for patients admitted the previous evening. If you hadn't grabbed coffee and some calories earlier, you waited until mid-day or later. Too bad.

At the conclusion of the workday, the last group activity was X-ray rounds. A middle-level resident designated as the clinic resident was in charge of making a list of the day's X-rays, gathering the films and transporting them to a viewing area where the entire team would view them in sequence.

If it was not too late in the day, we could find a radiologist to read the films with us. More often, they were gone by the time we gathered as a group. The intern or junior resident on duty that night would be responsible for recording the X-ray findings. We quickly learned to write them on a sticker to be pasted later in the patient's chart; quicker than taking notes to be copied into the chart. One step saved. Typed reports usually arrived one or two days later.

After X-ray rounds, operations performed during the day were discussed, any unstable patients were likewise brought to the attention of the on-duty team, and management was planned. Then the house officer on duty would proceed with any necessary scut work. Postoperative fevers triggered a standard evaluation: Culture everything: blood, sputum, urine; look at Gram stains of sputum and urine.We planted all the cultures and did the Gram stains ourselves—plus looked at the chest X-ray, inspected the wound, did the dressing care, and were available to talk with relatives during evening visiting hours.

I was once ripped apart by one of the more fascist chief residents for not getting a chest X-ray on a patient with an obvious urinary tract infection. "Don't think too much," I was told. "A good intern gets all the studies the chief will ask about."

The same chief resident opined that maggots were better than interns for debriding wounds, since they did not need time off to sleep.

After several ward service rotations, we developed the clinical wisdom to know that fevers were more common than not in the forty-eight hours after operation, particularly in heavy smokers, blood cultures were positive only in the rare patients with bacteremia, and wound inspections were almost always unrevealing for the first forty-eight hours after operation, so that dressings were best left in place for comfort.

We had all received a letter during intern orientation from the department chairmen expressing concern over the increasing number of emergency laboratory studies: "This excessive reliance on immediate and profuse laboratory help, save in exceptional circumstances, does not represent optimal medical practice."

In fact, laboratory support was very minimal during the nights and evenings. Only a few tests were available: blood sugar, BUN, potassium, amylase, barbiturate and salicylate levels, and blood gases. Total protein was available only on the pediatric service. We did much of the simple lab work ourselves: white blood counts, hematocrits, urinalyses, stool guaiacs for occult blood, Gram stains of sputum looking for bacteria. Most of these were simply done. The philosophy was that if it was important enough to order, the houseofficer should do it himself and have the results immediately.

Each service consisted of six house officers plus the chief resident, who had already finished the five years required for board eligibility and who was appointed for a one-year term. The chief residency was much sought after, and many residents would tread water in the research lab for six or twelve months before beginning the chief year. Most had taken a hiatus of two years in the military or the NIH research labs and had a respectable bibliography.

There was a senior resident each for the female and male side of the ward, and an intern for each as well. The night schedule was structured so that each intern was on call with the senior resident for his half of the service. A middle-level resident, called the *clinic resident* on the female side, was also in charge of X-rays. The first-year resident on the male side was called the *plastic resident* and was also responsible for the burn service and the private plastic surgery service.

Seemingly very structured, rigid continuity was provided because each intern and resident was familiar with the patients he cared for at night, as was the senior resident. We were on duty every other night, and in order for housestaff to have Saturday and Sunday off, we had to work Thursday and Friday. So we were on duty for five of seven nights, then off for the next five of seven nights. An intern starting duty at 7:00 a.m. on Saturday would probably not leave the hospital until after dinnertime on Monday.

In addition, the junior house officer on duty would make rounds on all his patients, address acute problems, retrieve the day's lab work, and write a progress note in the chart. Everything worked well unless there were emergency cases to be done—then two of the three residents on duty went to the operating room. Life lesson learned: Get all your work done early and quickly before it hits the fan. Reward: If you get your work done, you get to eat and sleep.

A high priority for the intern was "social service rounds"—a weekly conference with the nurses and social workers to discuss discharge planning. Operations that today are done on an outpatient basis or with minimal inpatient days then required several days of postoperative care in the hospital—seven days for a cholecystectomy or five or six for a hernia repair. We had a limited number of beds on our service, and patients could not be admitted for elective surgery unless a bed was available.

The logistical situation was explained very succinctly to the intern: "Your next hernia repair needs to be in that bed. Convince this family that papa needs to be placed in a nursing home!"

We provided superior patient care because there was always someone in the hospital who knew each patient, and we made both morning and evening rounds and discussed complicated patients as a group at the conclusion of the work day. A senior medical resident was our medical consultant and made morning rounds with us. They were exceptionally thorough and knowledgeable and taught us a great deal of internal medicine.

Total responsibility for patient care was assumed, and uninterrupted continuity was a given. We did not have a surgical ICU at the time and often kept critically ill patients in the recovery room. If necessary, the intern was expected to stay with the patient and manage fluid replacement, blood requirements, lab work, and frequent nasotracheal suctioning.

Needless to say, patients did not get much sleep in the recovery room; residents got even less if "up" with a sick patient. My "up record" was fifty-three consecutive hours. This standard of care I am sure was equaled in other sought-after residency programs but, to my knowledge, was not exceeded anywhere.

Years later, when governmental agencies thrust work hour limitations on us, Les Ottinger, our residency director, remarked that "tired and knowledgeable is considerably more to the patient's advantage than rested and ignorant."

Weekends were particularly arduous because we were required to rewrite all the patients' orders on Saturdays. In addition, the minimal weekday coverage by phlebotomists and IV nurses was not available. We worked cheaper than ancillary personnel, and the hospital knew as much. The intern needed to restart all IVs, draw all bloods, and prepare and dissolve antibiotics and other additives for intravenous infusions. This additional scut required about four or five additional hours on Saturday and Sunday mornings.

One could only hope that there were not an excessive number of emergency operations on both weekend nights. Fortunately, the emergency room schedule alternated for each service so that we were on call for only one of the two weekend nights. Nevertheless, many patients who entered were initially unstable and, after appropriate resuscitation and evaluation, would require surgery the following day or on Monday. Mondays were full days, culminating with X-ray rounds at the end of the day.

The intern was also required to prepare patients for operation. This preparation included sigmoidoscopies on all patients with elective hernias, and passing nasogastric tubes for patients requiring abdominal surgery since we did not trust anesthesia to do this without delaying the start of the operation. There was a Saturday morning vascular conference where we would discuss preoperative planning with the senior vascular surgeons. The house staff who had been on Thursday and Friday nights were expected to stay for the conference. Elective operations were scheduled on Saturday mornings as well.

Formal lectures and teaching exercises were virtually nonexistent because if lights were turned out to show slides, nearly everyone would fall asleep. The time when half the audience fell asleep was called the LD-50 for a lecture, so named after the pharmacology measure of drug toxicity—the dose that was lethal for 50% of the subjects. Besides, the visiting surgeons were too busy to present formal lectures to a small group.

Instead, teaching took place at conferences, where the intern would present preoperative patients to the visiting surgeons—an impressive totality of experience in one room. Using notes for your presentation was not done at the MGH because it showed that the intern did not know his patients well enough.

The senior surgeons "visited" only at the request of the residents and provided valuable experience and advice. Staff surgeons at the Mass General were called *visiting surgeons* rather than *attending surgeons*, stemming from a tradition going back to the nineteenth century, when hospitals were almost exclusively used to care for the indigent, often for terminal care.

The senior staff unanimously considered this assignment an honor and served without financial compensation. We had three visiting surgeons on the service at any given time, two junior and one senior. They were available upon invitation to provide consultation and advice and also to supervise the residents in the operating room.

Drs. Marshall K. Bartlett and Claude E. Welch,
the two senior MGH visiting surgeons, observing an
operation in the White Building from the viewing gallery.
(Courtesy of the Massachusetts General Hospital)

The two services had "visit rounds" and M & M conferences on Monday or Tuesday afternoons from 4:00 to 6:00 p.m. During the first hour we made rounds with the visiting surgeons and selected cases were presented, allowing the "visiting" surgeons to offer their advice. For the service having this exercise on Monday, it was called "black Monday" because ward work needed to be deferred until after the conferences. Until the work was done, the house officers who had been in the hospital since Saturday morning did not leave.

At the M & M conferences, which filled the second hour of "visit rounds", the senior residents presented details on any patient deaths or complications from the previous week. The format, devised by Ernest Codman at the beginning of the twentieth century, involved assigning each complication or death a grade: patient disease, error in technique, error in management, or error in judgment, abbreviated as PD, ET, EM, EJ. Patient disease indicated that nothing beyond the care provided would have allowed a more favorable outcome. The other categories were more censorious.

Score was kept. The senior and chief residents took the judgmental pronouncements quite seriously. Life lesson: You are always accountable.

Visiting surgeons were invited to help the residents in the operating room, depending on their own areas of interest and expertise. An MGH tradition was that a fairly senior visiting surgeon or another faculty member would "take an intern or junior resident through" an operation he was performing for the first time.

In actuality, the more senior surgeon directed the procedure step by step, providing the exposure, assuring that no untoward bleeding occurred, and directing the intern's every move. "Now cut here between my clamps."

The intern might be holding the scalpel and dictating himself as surgeon on the operative note, but the visiting surgeon was in fact running the show. Performing a major operation for the first time was a celebratory experience for a house officer.

"God, I'm good," you reflected. The adage was that surgery was not hard to do, it was hard to *get* to do.

A couple years later, when you are operating as a senior resident with an intern assisting, you realize that setting up exposure, dissecting correctly, and making all the myriad intraoperative decisions required to do an operation safely and well is not as easy as operating with a senior surgeon running interference. Such is experience. The more cerebral, nonsurgical medical specialists who think operative surgery is not cognitive have never helped a junior resident perform a major operation for the first time.

Everyone in the program was eager to operate. That is why we had chosen surgery as a specialty. Despite this goal, during the first half of the internship year, everyone was so overwhelmed with the scut work that we preferred to stay out of the operating room so we could get our floor work done. Without maximum efficiency, it was hard to get everything done and still be able to sleep for a few hours.

My first operation as a house officer was a tracheostomy performed under local anesthesia during my rotation on the anesthesia/ICU service. Later in the year, Dr. Paul Russell, the department chairman and a noted transplant surgeon, helped me with my first cholecystectomy. Dr. Howard Ulfelder, the chief of the gynecology service, helped with my first of several hysterectomies.

Operations were assigned to interns and junior residents by the chief resident, and this privilege was earned by taking care of sick patients in the middle of the night. It was not unusual for junior house officers to perform operations of major complexity that mandated a more senior resident in other programs.

With such a formidable workload, at one point, the chief of surgery queried the house staff about enlarging the intern class to lessen the workload. We unanimously preferred the more demanding workload to having our operative experience diluted among more individuals.

Needless to say, personal and family life were virtually nonexistent. I shared an apartment that was walking distance from the hospital with two medical school classmates: Reid Pitts, who became a prominent urologist at New York Hospital, and John Wesley, who ultimately became chief of pediatric surgery at the Mayo Clinic and U.C. Davis.

If we were on alternate schedules, we might not see each other for several months. Not until six or eight months into our internship year did we realize that the reason for our low rent was the absence of sunlight in our apartment because of surrounding tall buildings.

Fortunately, the most valuable amenity was a small grocery store on the first floor of our apartment building, where we bought dinner—usually a hoagie and a beverage—on our nights off. We also were surprised to discover the Beacon Chambers, a low-cost residence about 150 feet from our doorstep where many of the indigent and homeless we cared for in the emergency ward resided.

We had started internship with the expectation of being paid $3,600 for the twelve months of training. At that time, all the Boston hospitals had an identical fixed salary for interns and residents to avoid intercity financial competition for the most qualified house staff. Such an arrangement made sense then and now but would now obviously be illegal. A resident at another Boston hospital had two small children, successfully applied for welfare, and was chastised by his program director for bringing unwanted adverse publicity on the hospital.

To our surprise, just before the start of the academic year, the residents at the Boston City Hospital staged what was called a "heal-in" for better working conditions and compensation. At that time, the Boston City was a public hospital and the residents had exclusive authority to discharge patients. With the threat of patients not being discharged and the hospital being dangerously overcrowded, the city of Boston capitulated and raised residents' salaries to $6,000 per year. The other Boston hospitals followed suit.

We had all planned on surviving on $3,600 a year, made possible by the fact that we had minimal food, clothing, and automobile requirements and no time for recreation. Most single interns shared apartments. For those on duty, there was a free cafeteria meal at 10:00 p.m., which was often our only meal during the day, aside from the crackers and peanut butter in the surgeons' lounge. We quickly learned to sequester small containers of yogurt and fruit in our lockers for consumption the following day.

At the end of the year, my W2 form, which I still have in my possession, documented a salary of $2,400 for the six months from July to December—slightly less than one dollar per hour for our usual one hundred hour work week. Years later, George Zuidema, then the chair of surgery at Johns Hopkins, who had earned $1,500 a year as a resident, related that he had shared a cafeteria table with the current MGH associate director, who proudly proclaimed that they had hired a bright young administrative resident at an annual salary of $5,000. "You must remember that this man is a college graduate!" was the explanation.

Year earlier, Dr. John Knowles, director of the MGH when I was an intern, assured us that things were worse in days of yore ("When I was an intern ..."), as he recalled being paid $18.75 per month as an intern. "I was asked whether I wanted it in war bonds or cash!"

So we never complained about our remuneration. It was unmanly to complain about anything. We felt lucky to be where we were.

CHAPTER 4:   MORE INTERNSHIP

"Small operations for big problems don't work."

—W. Hardy Hendren

Our internship and first year of residency were a sort of unit. In addition to the ward service and ER, we all spent time on surgical subspecialties—pediatric surgery, urology, neurosurgery, gynecology, and anesthesia. Besides being the low man on the service, responsible for workups and scut, we learned something from each rotation: On neurosurgery, we learned how to evaluate unconscious patients and those with head trauma, on anesthesia we learned about airway management and ventilators, and on pediatric surgery we learned how to care for small and tiny patients with complicated problems.

Without question, the figure on the visiting staff who loomed larger than life for an intern was Dr. Hardy Hendren. Some men can throw a football fifty yards in the air. Some men can play ten chess matches simultaneously. Some can operate for twenty-four hours and still function at a high technical and intellectual level.

Hardy was this last type of person, earning him the nickname of "Hardly Human." Despite this nickname, he was extremely sensitive to the needs of his patients and to their families' fears and concerns.

Hardy excelled technically and chose one of the most challenging areas of pediatric surgery to perfect—complicated urogenital reconstructions. His two areas of expertise were megaureter, which occurs in both males and females, and cloaca deformities, which occur only in female infants.

Megaureter does not allow urine to pass freely from the kidneys to the bladder, predisposing patients to recurrent urinary infections and kidney damage.

Cloaca is a Latin word meaning "sewer," and babies born with cloaca deformities have multiple congenital abnormalities of the urinary tract, rectum, and vagina. The rectum, bladder, and vagina have a common opening, making hygiene a nearly insurmountable problem, even after performing a colostomy to divert stool.

Repair is exceptionally complex, and most surgeons would attempt to first reconstruct the rectum and then return later to reconstruct the bladder and vagina as a second operation. This was usually unsuccessful because of scarring and the difficulty of freeing up the repaired rectum safely from the remaining tissues and reconstructing a bladder and vagina.

Hardy was the only surgeon in the world who would attempt to do these repairs in one stage. The operation often required sixteen to twenty-four hours of uninterrupted operating room time and multiple technically difficult reconstructive procedures on small structures—preserving the anal sphincter, forming a neobladder, fashioning a vagina, and often repairing the uterus and ovaries as well. Hardy eventually performed about two hundred of these cloacal reconstructions, quickly gaining national and international acclaim for his unique expertise. He coined an aphorism that recurred in many of his lectures: "Small operations for big problems don't work."

Hardy loved to schedule a number of relatively small operations on Saturdays, when there would be fewer interruptive telephone calls. An intern was required to be available to assist on these, even on his weekend off. Although we alternated call with the pediatric intern, the intern in the operating room on Saturday was almost invariably the surgical intern, as most of the pediatric interns avoided the operating room like the plague.

One afternoon, while we were operating on a fairly complicated abdominal case, Hardy turned to me and said, "I wish you wouldn't do that."

I looked quickly at my retractor, to be sure it hadn't slipped; looked at my feet to be sure I was not standing on the suction tubing—negative to both.

"What did I do Hardy, what did I do?"

"You know what you did."

"No I don't, Dr. Hendren. Tell me what I did."

"You know what you did."

"Dr. Hendren, I really don't know what I did; tell me what I did and I won't do it again."

"You passed gas."

"No, I did not."

"Yes, you did. I'm the surgeon. I certainly would not do that. Leroy is the chief resident and he would not do that, and my Dorothy is the scrub nurse who has been with me for twenty-five years. She is a very gracious lady and she would not do that. You are the intern and obviously you are to blame."

At this juncture, I realized the smartest thing I could do was to shut up. At the MGH we learned that you are not only accountable for what you do, or don't do, but what people think you've done or not done.

Except that the word *accountability* meant blame. Someone must take the blame for everything, and it was almost always the lowest person on the totem pole. Fourth law of thermodynamics—shit flows downhill. Leave no 'tern unstoned, in MGH parlance. A bit later, we realized that Hardy had unknowingly nicked the cecum with a suture, causing a sudden feculent odor.

Hardy loved to have the house staff admire his technical virtuosity. One of my intern classmates, Josh Tofield, was a newly arrived surgical intern from Los Angeles. Josh was much less deferential and more laid back than most of the rest of us; so much so that we joked about him coming to Boston with a surfboard on his back. He trained in our plastic surgery residency after finishing the full five years of general surgery.

Most surgeons use a clamp to pass a silk ligature around a structure. Hardy used a Metzenbaum dissecting scissors. Grasp too hard and you cut the suture, too softly and you can't engage it. After watching Hardy, I imitated this technique, but could not duplicate his success rate.

One day, Hardy used the Metzenbaum scissors to tunnel the ureter obliquely through the bladder during a ureteral reimplant. "What do you think of that, California?" he asked Tofield, with a smile hidden under his OR mask.

"Not much, Kansas City!" was Tofield's reply. The senior resident laughed so hard he doubled over and contaminated his gloves. The anesthesiologist was said to have actually fallen off his stool and was on the floor holding his sides. The scrub nurse had tears running down her cheeks. When everyone calmed down, Hardy remarked, "Interns shouldn't oughta talk to professors of surgery that way, because on the phylogenetic scale, interns rank just below the flatworm."

Hardy was a unique individual from a Midwestern background, who interrupted his undergraduate studies at Dartmouth during World War II to join the Navy, where he trained as a fighter pilot. Fortunately or unfortunately, his training was ongoing when the war was winding down, and he was never sent to the Pacific.

Hardy was nevertheless determined to earn his wings as a carrier fighter pilot by perfecting his technique of carrier landings. These took place in the Gulf of Mexico. After Hardy had casually referred to his wartime service to the house staff, it became immortalized in successive resident skits.

"Hardy, who was fighting in the Gulf of Mexico in 1946?" was a frequent question. Hardy took this in good spirits.

After returning to Dartmouth with his bride, they lived in spartan apartments constructed south of the campus to accommodate returning veterans. Everyone found it difficult to make ends meet. Hardy showed his unusual initiative even then. When funds were insufficient, he devised several successful entrepreneurial ventures to do whatever was required to make ends meet economically. Good preparation for surgical excellence.

After receiving his undergraduate degree, Hardy attended Dartmouth Medical School, a two-year school at the time, and then transferred to Harvard for the two final years.

The intern matching program was almost finished in its development and about to be launched when Hardy was a fourth-year medical student. What is little known is his role in improving this program. Previously, students would apply to a multitude of hospitals, and the better students would receive multiple acceptances and were able to select at their leisure the hospital where they would train while other applicants waited until openings occurred. The new plan matched applicants and hospitals. Both listed their preferences; applicants learned where they would be going and hospitals learned their interns' names on the same day.

Hardy found the plan to have major imperfections and borrowed funds to improve it, incurring the anger of Harvard Dean George Packer Berry by attempting to fine-tune the plan already formulated. Hardy's improvements were accepted and have stood for more than forty years.

After graduating from Harvard, Hardy was matched with the Mass General Hospital, where he excelled as a general surgery resident. He continued his training in pediatric surgery as chief resident under Dr. Robert Gross at Boston Children's Hospital, finally finishing seven years of surgical training and then returning to the MGH as chief of pediatric surgery.

For approximately a decade, Hardy was the only pediatric surgeon at the MGH. Early on it was speculated that Hardy would eventually succeed Dr. Gross as chief of surgery at Children's Hospital, which he ultimately did.

One of the residents telephoned Hardy in the early morning to discuss a critically ill infant who had just undergone repair of a tracheo-esophageal fistula. The conversation was suddenly interrupted by several gunshots.

The resident was about to call the police when Hardy came back on the line, "I think I caught the little bastard that time. Goddamn those squirrels, they're all over my yard." Hardy later confessed to frequently shooting at squirrels from the back window of his home in Brookline.

Fast forward some eight years later, when I was a senior resident and had met my wife-to-be only a month previously. I introduced her to Hardy at the residents' change party. Now, when most people are introduced, they utter a perfunctory "How do you do" or "Glad to meet you." Not Hardy.

"I bet you wanted to meet me for a long time," he said. Esther asked me afterward who the hell this man was, and I simply had to reply that he was probably the best pediatric surgeon in the United States.

Hardy underwent major abdominal surgery several years later. A couple of days postop, when he was ready to begin a liquid diet, the residents taking care of him came to his room with three glasses and a bottle of choice Scotch.

Hardy's first activity upon hospital discharge was to go to his office, drop down on the floor, and do a series of push-ups to demonstrate to his staff that he really was healthy and fit to return to work.

The exemplary technical perfection that Hardy brought to his work as well his unequaled dedication to the care of children was an example to us all. This perfectionism did not stop in the operating room.

Fast forward to a couple of decades later yet. He and I were sitting together at a dinner of rack of lamb at an MGH reunion, and Hardy was quick to point out that he had cleaned the bones on his plate better than I had.

Old habits never die. Competitiveness does not stop in the operating room.

CHAPTER 5: PRIVATE SERVICE

Surgery is not hard to do, it's hard to get to do.

After twelve months of internship, we became junior residents. Twelve months wrought an extraordinary change. We knew no fear. We were the iron men. We had survived internship.

Rotations on the private service, like all others, were for two months. We did not work on the private service until our second year in the program, when we were capable of making daily rounds alone on a large census of patients and providing pre- and postoperative care with minimal supervision from the senior staff. We all had multiple rotations on the private service in the four years after internship.

The private service consisted of six "teams." Some of these were historical group practices, which had gradually added individuals and seen the retirement or demise of older surgeons. Some of the more senior surgeons had their own instruments and employed their own nurses, who would be sure that these instruments were available, and return to the surgeon's office after the OR schedule was done to help with office patients.

*MGH Visiting Surgeons, circa 1967. The surgical
staff expanded considerably in subsequent years.
(Courtesy of the Massachusetts General Hospital)*

Other teams segregated patients with specific problems, such as vascular, thoracic, or endocrine. A resident assigned to a given service knew which senior surgeons he would be working with, and what sort of issues the patients would have.

Team one was the "Allen team," and along with team two concentrated on gastrointestinal surgery. Dr. Allen had been an illustrious chief of the east surgical service and had gradually recruited other individuals to join him. During my residency, the senior surgeon was Dr. Claude E. Welch, known to the residents as "Claudius." He had been president of many surgical societies, including the American College of Surgeons and the American Surgical Association, and was consulted when the pope was shot in 1982. He wrote four textbooks and several hundred scientific papers.

Dr. Welch was a technically able and versatile surgeon. He had an encyclopedic knowledge of the surgical literature. He and Dr. Wyland Leadbetter were the only private surgeons who routinely made daily rounds with their residents.

Dr. Welch started at about 6:30 a.m. on the top floor of the Baker Building, and his assumption was that the resident had already made rounds on the entire service, written orders, changed dressings, scrutinized laboratory work, and made any necessary management decisions, allowing Dr. Welch to move quickly.

Several years later, Dr. Welch's service was my first assignment upon returning from the military with a new bride and an infant son, neither of whom I saw very much of during this rotation, since I needed to be in the hospital at about 5:00 a.m. to start my rounds. A rather rude awakening after two years of rather leisurely existence as an army surgeon.

One of the residents tried to convince Dr. Welch that it would be more efficient if they rounded together at 6:30, allowing the resident to defer work rounds until after the day's operating was finished. Dr. Welch listened patiently and seemed to agree. But he merely acquiesced, and said, "Uh huh," his frequent response to a variety of questions.

It subsequently became clear when Dr. Welch asked about current lab work and updates that he still expected the resident to have made work rounds prior to 6:30 a.m. In his autobiography, *A Twentieth Century Surgeon,* he described rounding in the same way for Dr. Arthur Allen, whom he had joined in practice after residency. Some things never change.

Dr. Welch was often accompanied by a small entourage of visitors, residents working in research labs, or guests eager to avail themselves of his wisdom. One of the residents invited them to join him in the "pre-round" work rounds at 4:30 a.m., when there would be more time to discuss the patients in detail. None ever accepted the invitation. Many nevertheless claimed afterward that they had worked with Dr. Claude Welch at the MGH.

"The shortest distance between two points is to follow Dr. Welch making rounds." His postoperative patients and patients he had seen in consultation were located in no fewer than two and as many as four buildings within the hospital, and he had an uncanny knack of knowing every back corridor, staircase, construction blockage, and elevator.

The resident would quickly present each patient to him. He made few comments and spent little time talking with patients, yet they were nevertheless in awe of him. Dr. Welch could tell patients in just a few words that they had incurable cancer, and the patient would almost invariably be effusive in his thanks. He was sometimes known as "the grey ghost" because it was alleged that he could simultaneously back out of a patient's room while entering it.

The annual meeting of the American College of Surgeons took place during my rotation, and Dr. Welch was the president that year. Several of the patients knew that he would be away presiding at the meeting; one or two of them asked if they could call him with questions. His usual response followed, "Dr. Jarrett will take care of any questions you have."

An occasional patient would prefer someone other than the resident to change his dressing or remove his sutures. Dr. Welch had a knack of ignoring these requests.

"Dr. Welch, I want you to take out my stitches, not anyone else."

A quick nod from Dr. Welch. "Dr. Jarrett will take them out." Snip, snip, snip. Done.

He had a large following within New England and a good part of the northeastern United States. During one of my rotations as the emergency room senior resident, Dr. Welch's son John was my intern. I asked him to work up a patient who had been transferred to his father's service from Cape Cod. To our mutual amusement, the patient said, "My goodness, Dr. Welch, I thought you would be a much older man!"

Dr. Welch and Dr. Marshall Bartlett usually operated in the Phillips House in adjoining operating rooms. They were among a small group of surgeons who employed their own scrub nurses, who worked in their offices when not in the operating room, and who cleaned and transported their personal instruments to and from the OR.

The resident was challenged to keep up with Dr. Welch's almost unique ability to never waste time. He was never seen drinking coffee or chatting in the lounge between cases. He used any free time to check on patients in the hospital or run back to his office to work on some writing.

At the end of the operation, the resident would secure the patient's dressing and escort him to the recovery room, write the postoperative orders, and then frantically race back to begin the next case. It was a point of honor for the resident to move quickly enough to not let Dr. Welch prep and apply the sterile drapes around the operative field, which he frequently did, after mopping the floor and wheeling the patient from the holding area to the operating room.

The instant at least some of the sterile drapes were in place, he would move ahead, grab a scalpel from the instrument stand his nurse had not fully arranged, and have the incision made before the rest of the team was in place and ready.

One of the strengths of the MGH program was that there were relatively few visiting surgeons, each of whom had unique skills and expertise. During the course of the residency, we usually had an opportunity to work with all of them, and they each affected our training in different ways.

The senior resident on the private service was called the scoutmaster. His task was to schedule the residents to assist on the day's cases—sometimes a very difficult management task as multiple cases were in progress, emergencies were added, and when a case would finish and allow the following case to start was obviously unpredictable. The custom was that the resident on a given team had his choice of whom to scrub with, but he was expected to assist the senior surgeon on that team, unless there was a more major case scheduled by one of the other surgeons.

We were on duty every other night, alternating with the same resident each time, so that we were covering our own team plus another and got to know the patients on both fairly thoroughly. We depended on the resident we alternated with to take care of any problems that arose during the night—fevers, postoperative complications, diagnostic issues. If this was not done, we arrived in the morning expecting to go to the operating room and had to somehow address these issues between operations. We needed to know that someone had our back on our nights off.

The patients were not as sick and complicated as those we were used to caring for on the ward service, as most had been admitted for elective operations. There was more support from ancillary personnel, and thus less scut work. Nevertheless, each resident was running a service alone, and hence was also the *de facto* intern.

One of the least popular tasks was hanging blood. The MGH had a rule that only IV nurses and residents could retrieve units of blood from the blood bank, bring them to the patients' bedside and connect them to the IV. And the IV nurses were not on duty at night.

"Mrs. Smith's blood is ready!" would be the telephone call that awakened and sent you to the blood bank.

There was an assumption that a half-sleeping resident could bring the blood to the correct patient more safely than a fully awake nurse. Fortunately, there were no transfusion mismatches that I knew of. If two units of blood had been ordered, every resident tried to get the nurses to let him hang both simultaneously. Rarely successful. Another call two hours later: "The second unit of blood is ready!"

Most of the private operating was done in the two old operating rooms in the Phillips House, which were rather primitive, and the five operating rooms on the eleventh floor of the Baker Building, which was somewhat better but still antiquated. Dr. Welch wrote to the hospital director at about this time and described these ORs as "hardly better than those of the Middle Ages." The White Building ORs were reserved for the ward services, and it was not until the Grey Building was constructed that the ORs were consolidated.

Weekends on the private service were particularly onerous because there were a large number of Sunday admissions for operation on Monday. The resident's job was to do the history and physical examination, which was handwritten in the chart in the days before a dictation system. He would then draw the blood for the preoperative lab work, do the cardiogram, and order a chest X-ray.

At the end of the day, he would round again, write a preoperative note summarizing the preoperative diagnosis, the lab work, his reading of the cardiogram, and the chest X-ray.

Every hospital has its gold coast, preferred by well-to-do patients because the rooms are more spacious, the meals usually better, and the nurses are caring for fewer patients. We had the Phillips House, built in 1907 overlooking the Charles River. Many of the rooms had fireplaces. Some originally had small anterooms where servants could sleep. S.S. Pierce would deliver food if the patient wished. We used to say that the Phillips House was close to a good hospital.

We also had Phillips House nurses. They were very kind and solicitous to the patients. Some were very knowledgeable and contributed to patient care as valuable team members. After a thoracotomy, the quantity of drainage from the chest tube placed to evacuate fluid and air was closely watched, because excessive drainage suggested that the patient was bleeding and needed to be reexplored. One nurse observed that a chest tube warm to the touch was draining enough to require the patient to be reexplored, thereafter known as "Sheila's sign."

But in general, we were convinced that a nurse had to be beyond retirement age to work in the Phillips House. These nurses generated a host of Phillips House stories that I initially did not believe. Two things were said of these stories: First, no one who had not been an MGH surgical resident believed them; second, they were all true.

Enter the residents' change party skits, starring the MGH broad heavies, named after the stout dissecting scissors used in the OR and portrayed by a duo of the stouter, more hirsute residents in the program. This pair made semiannual appearances in the skits. One was too nearsighted to be able to read the dial on the blood pressure cuff; the other was too deaf to hear through the stethoscope. Together, as a team, they took blood pressures.

Any good surgical resident develops specific subconscious reflexes that help prevent disasters and occasionally save lives. One reflex was to proceed directly to the Phillips House when the nurse's question about a patient did not make sense, which was often the case. When paged by a Phillips House nurse saying, "This patient doesn't look good," we knew to go directly to the patient's floor, to not pass go, and address a potential catastrophe of unknown kind.

One famous such call was about a patient who "didn't look good" after a lung resection. He was blue and having obvious trouble breathing. His chest tube had a large clamp across it and the suction had been turned off.

"What the hell is going on here?"

"I turned the suction off because the noise was keeping the patient awake," the nurse answered. Luckily the situation was remedied easily, removing the clamp, turning the suction back on, allowing the lung to reexpand. Tragedy averted.

One of the residents required operation for a popliteal artery entrapment, a rare cause of arterial disease in young patients, and in his case causing enough damage to the artery that a short vein bypass graft needed to be done. The standard postop nursing instructions after an arterial bypass were to check the pulses below the bypass every one or two hours for the first day to be sure the graft had not occluded. The resident, now a patient in the Phillips House, overheard his nurse telling another, "I can't feel a foot pulse, but his radial pulse is seventy-two, so he must be okay."

One team found a patient in cardiac arrest during rounds. (The Phillips House was not where you wanted your patient to be with an emergency.) The nurse was asked to get a tray to put under the patient for CPR.

"I can't doctor; they're all set up for dinner."

"Forget dinner and get a damn tray," replied the senior resident. Another nurse who had overheard the conversation appeared with a calling card tray, sterling silver, about six by nine inches in size.

The emergency ward resident, one of whose jobs was to field outside telephone calls for medical advice, was called by a man who said, "My toes are turning black and nobody has looked at them in days!"

"Sir, you should come into the hospital and let us look at them."

"I am *in* the hospital; I'm a patient in the Phillips House."

One resident was paged directly by a patient in the Phillips House who complained, "I can't wake my private duty nurse and she doesn't respond." Sure enough, when the resident arrived, the nurse was slumped in a chair and could not be resuscitated.

As a junior resident, I initially didn't believe some of these tales either.

The next step up in the economic and social hierarchy from Phillips House nursing was a "special." For an extra daily hospital charge and with your doctor's order, the hospital would provide a private-duty nurse, nicknamed a "special," who cared solely for her one assigned patient.

They were very kind, dutiful, and attentive to comfort amenities, including giving backrubs and making tea and coffee for visitors. Most considered a "special" nursing assignment as an invitation to tunnel vision and permission to abjure any knowledge or interest in anything but their assigned patient. They were not very helpful with sick, complicated postop patients, to whom they were occasionally assigned. One resident, lacking a wristwatch, asked a special nurse for the time.

"I'm sorry doctor, I'm a special nurse."

I was on duty the night Robert Kennedy was shot, and the first thing I did before starting rounds in the Phillips House the next morning was to ask the first nurse I saw if he was still alive. "I don't know, doctor. I'm Mr. Smith's special."

I became a believer.

CHAPTER 6: EMERGENCY WARD

"Every person has at least three surgical
diseases. All you have to do is find them."

—Michael Crichton, *Five Patients*

None of the residents liked the emergency ward (known as "the pit") very much because there was no operating involved, merely preparing a large number of very sick patients for other surgeons to operate on.

I had spent two months in the emergency ward as an intern, and I learned a great deal—mostly suturing lacerations, working up preoperative patients, and learning to evaluate patients with maximal speed and efficiency.

I returned as a senior resident a couple of times over the next few years. At the time, the MGH had no ER physicians or residents, nor any thoracic, plastic, gynecology, ENT, cardiac, or vascular residents. We did most of the head and neck cancer surgery. Orthopedics, urology, and neurosurgery had separate services and residency programs, but we usually were required to evaluate their patients first before calling in another specialty.

The general surgery resident was it. It was great experience, and taught us to be good general physicians, resourceful and efficient with time management. But being the EW senior was a higher level of responsibilities with new challenges.

I am convinced that our care was better than that in most non-trauma-center EWs today because we had "top-down" triage—the most senior resident saw the patient first and initiated diagnostic studies and treatment. This practice obviated the several hours of waiting time for semi-emergent patients, which is currently the norm in most EWs today, and yet allowed us to move with great speed for major life-threatening emergencies—cardiogenic shock, ruptured aneurysms, and gunshot wounds.

The resident I was replacing briefed me the day before I started.

"You know the drill; twenty-four hours on, twenty-four off. For half your shift, you're the gauleiter (MGH vernacular for EW senior resident). You see all the patients first, draw the bloods, send them off, start the IV, do the cardiogram yourself and check it, order the chest film. Then triage them; if they're medical, call the medical HO to get started on the admission workup. The medical interns all carry little black bags and take at least two hours to do an admission workup. Call the other services down for their admissions. Remember that some of them are hard to get to come, but you have the authority to admit the patient directly to their service. You may have to threaten bodily harm to move things along."

"Sounds good."

"The other twelve hours, you're the surgical senior. Do the workups as fast as you can. Watch the intern."

"Wonderful. I can't wait." No extra charge for sarcasm.

"If the patient needs to be operated on, call the senior on the floor, but make sure everything's been done; otherwise, he'll chew your ass."

"Got it." Some of the senior residents were more toxic than others.

"Keep things moving. Don't let the interns make a meal of suturing a laceration. Get everyone buffed up during the night, otherwise you won't be able to leave in the morning."

We had a very active emergency ward, serving a variety of the community's needs and seeing approximately 200 patients per day. Until my last year of residency, we saw relatively little major trauma, as most were taken to the Boston City Hospital. We did see a large indigent population and a large number of alcoholics, many with GI bleeding. The ER was run by the residents. Staff physicians would occasionally appear if one of their patients was being admitted.

Because the senior resident was more experienced than the other house staff, he could dispense with self-limited problems and arrange for patient follow-up very quickly.

A major problem in any emergency room is the backlog of patients waiting to be seen. Too many patients waiting is a brewing catastrophe because the sudden arrival of a critically ill and complicated patient could require the attention of all three surgical residents. The major problem for the surgical triage resident in the emergency room was getting the medical service to move quickly. The tradition was that the medical intern would do the admission workup, most commonly for pneumonia, cardiac problems, uncontrolled diabetes, or stroke. These workups were three to four handwritten pages, and when done well and thoroughly, were enormously time-consuming.

The medical service practice was that after the intern finished the workup, he would call the house officer on the destination floor, who would come down and repeat the entire scenario before transporting the patient from the EW. This may have provided an enhanced learning experience on the medical service because two house officers did the workup, but it resulted in rooms being tied up for several hours, making it difficult for the triage resident to move things along.

We had two residents and an intern assigned to the emergency ward at any given time, attached to either the east or west surgical service. Rounds would start at 7:00 a.m., and the residents would present the patients to the senior and chief residents on the service. Many patients could be admitted to the overnight ward adjacent from the EW for up to seventy-two hours for stabilization and further evaluation. The policy was that patients with chest pain or pulmonary problems were evaluated by medicine and patients with abdominal problems were evaluated by surgery.

At that time, the need for operation was indeterminate for many patients with gastrointestinal bleeding or abdominal pain. The intern's task was to obtain hematocrits or white counts every six or eight hours to follow the patient's progress. We did this lab work by hand, which allowed results to be more timely than if the work was sent to the laboratory. We were also aware that house staff labor was cheaper than hiring more lab techs.

We were not allowed to leave the EW during our twenty-four-hour shift. When you tried to get a few hours' sleep, you might find an empty litter in the minor trauma room or a bed in the overnight ward. If not, you stayed in the EW residents' office off the registration desk. In either case, constant loudspeaker announcements allowed only short-duration sleep.

After making rounds, we were required to stabilize the patients before leaving the hospital. If the senior residents on our floor were both going to the operating room, one of the emergency room residents had to stay in place until someone was out of the OR to deal with the emergencies. Our work week was in excess of ninety hours. In contrast to other rotations, where we could usually catch a few hours' sleep, we were often up for twenty-four consecutive hours.

Although the triage resident could assign a patient to a given service for admission, the receiving service might dispute this decision if they thought they were too busy, or if they thought the patient's needs were better handled by someone else. Sending a complicated or demanding patient to another service was called a *dump* or a *turf,* and the residents had ingenious ways for determining when another service should be responsible for the patient.

For example, a patient with vague abdominal pain who might or might not require operation could sometimes be turfed to the medical service if he was diabetic and his diabetes was not under control. Likewise, chronic lung disease, which was almost universal in our patient population, was another reason to turf a patient to medicine. Having the patient on another service cut down our workload.

But there was a drawback. Internists are thinkers and are thorough, but they are procrastinators. Surgeons come from the tradition of barbers—they are action-oriented. You did not want a patient on the medical service if quick decision making or ongoing attention to blood transfusion or fluid balance requirements were needed. Welch and Hedberg wrote, "The medical ward remains one of the most hazardous places for the patient who develops peritonitis."

The competition between the east and west surgical services for patients was longstanding and intense, as everyone wanted to maximize his operative experience. There were very specific and rigid rules concerning service designation to the two surgical services.

If a patient came to the emergency room with pneumonia and one service had put a consult note in the chart, that patient then "belonged" to that service for a specified period of time. If the patient was admitted to medical ward and then followed by surgeons with progress notes in the chart, that patient then "belonged" to the respective surgical service for a longer period, usually several months.

"Drop a note on every med admission with pneumonia. They may need a bronch, and maybe a thoracotomy."

The surgical service did most of the necessary workups, including spinal taps, arteriograms, and endoscopies. We had a separate endoscopy rotation where we performed a large number of bronchoscopies and esophagogastroscopies with help from experienced visiting surgeons. Colonoscopy was just beginning to be available when I was a resident.

What was particularly difficult was getting the resident on certain specialty services to see and admit a patient. Most notorious was the psychiatry service where the residents were loath to see a patient and even less likely to do an admission workup after 3:00 p.m.

The triage resident had a certain latitude in this area and if necessary could admit a patient to a given service, write orders, and notify the unavailable or unwilling resident after the fact. I once called the psychiatry resident to see a fifty-year-old lady who was suicidal. This was, and is, almost a mandatory requirement for hospital admission.

"Just give her 200 mg of Thorazine every six hours, and I can see her in the clinic in about two weeks." This was a large dose of Thorazine, almost guaranteed to put the patient to sleep, if not render her unconscious.

I called the resident back about an hour later and said, "We have a twenty-two-year-old nymphomaniac college girl ..."

"I'll be right down." He arrived a few short minutes afterward.

"I'm sorry, but the nymphomaniac college student signed out against advice. While you're here, maybe you could see the fifty-year-old suicidal lady."

What followed was a tirade starting with "You son of a bitch," followed by multiple F-bombs. Thus I first learned about anger management and understood why psychiatrists often provide counseling for it.

As with everything else, the standards of performance were very high. The EW residents' lounge had several typewriters, and after some of the residents began typing their workups, it quickly became the expected standard for all workups to be typewritten, as well as the daily progress notes for patients admitted to the overnight ward.

On one occasion, a patient arrived with a complicated gastric problem. He had undergone several operations in Italy, details unknown to him. I managed to place a call to Rome, find his surgeon, and have him read the operative note to an Italian translator at my side. With a specific appreciation of what had been done before, I presented the patient on rounds the next morning, expecting generous kudos. None were forthcoming. This was the expected level of care.

Some of the telephone referrals that the gauleiter took were bizarre, and we quickly became used to some of the less knowledgeable physicians in Boston. One notorious doctor had a triple-threat reputation: his diagnoses were almost always wrong, his patients were always very sick, and he was usually patronizing with the residents. He was the only general practitioner in Charlestown and had a large practice.

"I have a real fascinoma for you high-powered Harvard guys."

"Yes, sir."

"I have a young albino boy with a seizure disorder. Maybe you guys can figure it out. Might be a CPC for the New England Journal."

Thirty minutes later a pale, young, red-headed boy was brought in by his parents and promptly collapsed when he stood at the desk to give his identifying information. Diagnosis: red-headed boy was bleeding and hypovolemic had a treacherously low blood count, and fainted when standing.

We were also *de facto* physicians to the North End mob. They were usually grateful patients but not too bright, but could not be moved from their explanations, often very original, of why they came to the EW. They never knew who shot them.

"What happened to you, Tony?"

"I dunno, Doc. I was walking down the street minding my own business and I had pain in my right foot."

"Tony, you've a through and through gunshot wound of the foot!"

"No shit, Doc. Good thing I came in."

"Tony, how come there's no bullet hole in your shoe?"

"Dunno, Doc."

The EW rotation gave us a chance to interface with residents on other services and to do one-on-one teaching with the medical students on their surgery rotation, some of whom were outstanding. The surest way, then and now, of being accepted for a highly competitive surgical internship was to distinguish yourself as a medical student by working longer hours than your peers, helping the intern with his workload by accepting more scut, and being identified as more reliable than your classmates.

The students who looked upon their surgery rotation as merely a passive learning experience usually did not go into surgery, got to do fewer minor procedures, and were not treated particularly warmly by the overworked resident team.

During my rotation as ER senior, there appeared an exceptionally tall medical student who hung around the periphery most of the time.

"Who is that tall student who keeps hanging around here? Is he on medicine?"

"He's an HMS (Harvard Medical Student) doing an elective here, writing a book about the MGH."

"Christ! The HMS electives get flakier and flakier every year. Why doesn't he roll up his sleeves, do some workups, have us show him how to suture, and do minor procedures?"

From this elective, the late Michael Crichton wrote *Five Patients,* a book about the MGH and medical care at the end of the 1960s. He later wrote *The Andromeda Strain, Jurassic Park, The Great Train Robbery,* and more than a dozen excellent novels.

Michael never really wanted to be a doctor, and each year during medical school equivocated about continuing but was persuaded to do so by his advisors and deans. He was one of those uniquely talented, exceptionally bright individuals who would have made an impact in any field he chose.

Five Patients contains vignettes about the MGH and its teaching programs, as well as the author's opinions about medical care. He quotes a surgical resident admonishing, "Every person has at least three surgical diseases. All you have to do is find them." Some of his thoughts are trenchant, but some have not stood the test of time. He wrote, "neither television nor the computer has made much difference yet to routine hospital functioning."

Michael's observation ultimately proved to be incorrect, but my initial judgments likewise did not have a high accuracy rate.

CHAPTER 7:   WARD SERVICE

The bad thing about being on duty every other night is that you miss half the operations.

We continued with rotations of two months each. The middle years had less operating than everyone desired, but we had increasing responsibilities, particularly in the outpatient clinics. Contrary to what we believed, nonoperative outpatient clinic rotations required a considerable amount of mature judgment in evaluating patients and managing diagnostic evaluations. At that time, patients could be admitted to the hospital for diagnostic studies and workup and at the same time enhancing our teaching mission. No longer.

The senior residency was not one year of major responsibility, but two, including a great deal of operating. Residents did not have identical rotations because it was not possible for everyone to have a rotation on each service but each of us had an experience tailored to our individual goals and needs. The department made an effort to accommodate interests in cardiothoracic, vascular, pediatric, and transplant surgery with senior rotations in these areas. We also had rotations at two community hospitals near Boston and a senior rotation in thoracic surgery in Great Britain. We remained eager to operate as much as possible.

The resident-run ward services were in competition with the visiting surgeons for operative experience. While the house staff did all the operating on the ward service, we did only a tiny fraction of the surgery on the private service, so that we had a vested interest in the ward service being as busy as possible.

Jerry Austen was concerned about preserving the autonomy of the resident-run ward services at a time when more and more patients had private insurance and could insist on being admitted to a private physician or surgeon if they so desired. Many of the patients we admitted for emergency operations from the emergency ward had private insurance but were content enough with our initial care that they chose not to be transferred to the private surgeons.

Dr. Austen helped us by providing the senior residents with business cards with our names and the page operator's telephone number. We were encouraged to wear neckties rather than hospital whites. When called to the EW by the junior resident, we would introduce ourselves as the surgeon on call (which I guess we were, technically). Only if questioned further would we admit to being the resident, not the staff surgeon.

Not only did we need to compete with the visiting surgeons for operating, but with our own colleagues as well. The senior and chief residents traditionally helped the junior house staff in the operating room. Some were hungrier than others and could not resist the temptation to take over—known as "escalating the case"—which often occurred if the junior house officer put down his scissors to ask for a different instrument or a sponge. I developed what we called the "Big Daddy move," palming the dissecting scissors to prevent the chief resident with this nickname from escalating.

The east and west services remained enormously competitive with each other, as they had been since their creation in 1874. The west service chief resident had lapel buttons made saying "West is Best." There were strict rules of service designation (read *patient possession*) for consultations seen on other services. Often unsolicited surgical consultations were provided when the resident heard of a particularly interesting patient on another service.

When we gathered for X-ray rounds in the late afternoon, there was a "cheat sheet" that the radiology resident left after scrutinizing the day's X-rays and listing the patients' names and brief diagnoses. The intention was to assist resident teams who came to the X-ray department in the late afternoon after the radiology residents had departed, which was much earlier than medical and surgical residents did.

A not infrequent occurrence was for the senior residents to troll the diagnoses on the cheat sheet and then appear uninvited on the medical wards, see a particularly interesting patient, and write a consultation note, thus branding the patient as belonging to the east or west service.

One day, we were in a more frivolous mood than usual, and the chief resident suggested we construct a sham cheat sheet, listing fictitious patients on the medical service with diagnoses intended to provoke major interest, if not salivation, on the other service: large substernal goiter, proximal gastric carcinoma, aorto-iliac aneurysm. This bait was left conspicuously behind to be discovered by the east chief resident, who sent his senior resident to the Bulfinch Building with unequivocal orders to "find these patients and write notes on them."

Naturally, nonexistent patients were never found, despite a good deal of time spent. In this case, the senior resident (Andy Warshaw) became president and the chief resident (Joe Fischer) chairman of the board of regents of the American College of Surgeons, and respectively were surgery department chairman at the MGH and at Cincinnati.

On another occasion, we posed a mockup of the picture of the first demonstration of ether, which was hanging outside the Ether Dome, now a national historic monument. I was the patient, our scrub nurse was present, as was the chief resident. Among the spectators were three future surgery department chairmen. We hung the finished photo surreptitiously outside the Ether Dome, where it still remains several decades later.

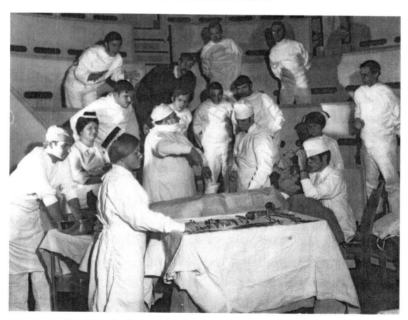

Satirical photo of first use of ether at the MGH.
We posed this photo in the Ether Dome in 1971. I
was the patient. Three future surgery department
chairmen are in the group. (Courtesy of the author)

Aside from rare episodes of frivolity, the ward service was an intensely serious undertaking. We prided ourselves on our independence and the sophistication and quality of our surgical care.

We had two Rhodes scholars in our residency program, and the medical residency had two more. We were aware of the strong tradition of excellence and innovation on the resident-run service.

Just a few years before us, in 1962, the first limb reimplantation was performed by a four-resident team led by Ron Malt, the chief resident on duty that night. Robert Shaw, a gifted vascular surgeon, led the surgical team, spent the night in the operating room with Malt, and graciously gave credit to him for leading the team and declining to transfer the patient to his private service.

Some of the residents made enormously innovative contributions above and beyond what one would expect in mid-training. At that time, we did the majority of the head and neck cancer surgery. These patients were often terribly sick and had major comorbidities because of tobacco use and alcoholism. If radiation was required for their tumors, significant healing problems often eventuated, causing oral-cutaneous and esophagocutaneous fistulas, which were refractory to operative closure.

Dr. Jim May was an exceptionally polite Kentuckian who later became chief of plastic surgery at the MGH and president of the American Board of Plastic Surgery. On rounds one morning when he was an intern the chief resident asked him to explain why a postoperative patient had alternating periods of anuria (no urine output) and copious urine output.

"Sir, I think the patient has a bladder diverticulum which fills by gravity but does not empty when the patient is positioned on his side with the diverticulum dependent. When the nurses turn him to the opposite side, the diverticulum empties and the urine output improves."

First, we had to convince Jim that the intern was not expected to address the chief resident as *sir*, and then that the patient's urine issue was likely intermittent hypovolemia which responded to increased IV fluids.

A couple of years later, when Jim was the plastic surgery resident and had just returned from a year in Australia learning the then-nascent techniques of microvascular surgery, we had a patient with an esophagocutaneous fistula refractory to treatment.

Jim proposed taking a segment of jejunum from the abdomen and connecting its blood supply under the microscope to the neck arteries. A free tissue transfer procedure had not been done before at the MGH, and I believe there were only one or two successful attempts elsewhere. The rest of us were skeptical of the chances for a successful outcome.

None of the visiting plastic or vascular surgeons had prior experience with microvascular surgery at that time, but Jim felt he could do the procedure, which he did without difficulty, with the encouragement and support of one of the senior plastic surgeons. Because of trepidation about eventual healing, the jejunal segment in the neck was temporarily covered with a skin graft before being connected to the esophagus. After its viability was ascertained, continuity was reestablished and the fistula resected. The patient did well thereafter and was able to swallow and return to a normal lifestyle.

Ben Cosimi was another talented resident who had been a medical student at the University of Colorado under transplant pioneer Dr. Tom Starzl. At that time, acute postoperative renal failure was usually fatal because of limited experience with hemodialysis, which was just beyond its infancy at the time and not available on a large scale.

If patients with postop renal failure could be supported with dialysis for ten or fourteen days, their kidneys could often recover and function on their own. The MGH had one dialysis machine, which was controlled by the nephrology service, who limited its use to their own renal patients.

The west service had a critically ill patient in acute renal failure after resection of a ruptured abdominal aneurysm, emergency bowel resection, and colostomy creation. The judgment was that he would die if not afforded dialysis. The nephrology service refused to do so.

Ben Cosimi and Judah Folkman, the west chief resident, took the latter's station wagon to a few junk yards and returned with an old washing machine and sundry other parts, which Ben made into a functional dialysis machine over the weekend. Sterile tubing and coils were obtained from Baxter Labs, and the patient was successfully dialyzed, saving his life.

When the nephrologists were asked to see him again, they were so angered that the surgical service had invaded their turf that they vowed to never again provide consultations to the west surgical service. The hemodialysis unit nevertheless remained part of the department of surgery until 1995.

Ben Cosimi stayed at the MGH as chief of the transplant service and professor of surgery at Harvard; Judah Folkman became chief of surgery at Children's Hospital at age thirty-four and pioneered research in tumor angiogenesis, was winner of the ACS's Jacobson award, and was mentioned as a potential Nobel laureate before his untimely death.

One day a young, extremely attractive woman entered the emergency room and was told that she had an acute appendicitis and would require appendectomy. She became panicky and hysterical and insisted that the right lower quadrant scar, however small, would interfere with her livelihood as a go-go dancer.

The senior resident at time, John B. Mulliken, was planning a career in plastic surgery and confessed to the intern that he had been planning a strategy for this situation for quite some time. They assured the patient that she would have almost no scar and would be satisfied with her cosmetic outcome.

Mulliken raised a flap in the right lower quadrant, leaving its pedicle attached, and performed the appendectomy through the bed of the flap. The peritoneum was closed, the flap replaced in its original position, and buried sutures and Steri-Strips were used to achieve an optimal cosmetic result. The patient was so pleased that she invited the resident team to a special performance at her club—a rare treat in the midst of our call schedule.

Dr. Michael DeBakey wrote that the three unsolved problems of surgery were suction, lighting, and anesthesia. We addressed the first two, but the last remained a problem.

For the first few decades of the hospital's existence, there was no anesthesia. Patients were given brandy and opium for pain, and assistants held them down during operations. John Collins Warren believed that complete muscular relaxation was necessary to reduce a dislocated hip; a tobacco enema caused the patient to become hypotensive from nicotine toxicity and the necessary relaxation ensued. The number of operations that could be done was very few until anesthesia became available about the middle of the nineteenth century, yet it remained primitive by our standards and was not administered by specifically trained personnel.

When I started as an intern, the anesthesia coverage in the evenings and nights was very spotty. A sole anesthesia resident was in-house and administered anesthesia for our patients. There was no in-house backup at the attending level. I do not recall an attending anesthesiologist ever being present at night.

Enter the skits we produced twice a year for the change party celebrating the chief residents finishing their year. We were short on singing and dramatic talent and even shorter on time needed to rehearse, but we had an abundance of issues to satirize and people to roast. The anesthesia service and their residents' lack of English language fluency were among the most frequent subjects.

The recurring skit involved a surgeon complaining about his patient not being fully asleep, inadequately ventilated, or some other intraoperative anesthesia misadventure. Repeated complaints shouted by the surgeon over the ether screen did not elicit a response. Finally a head appears, "No speakee English!" The crowd roars.

One year, Jerry Austen brought Dr. Richard Kitz to the party. Kitz had just arrived from Columbia-Presbyterian in New York to become chairman of the anesthesia department. Kitz was appalled and probably somewhat offended by the satire directed against his department but shortly thereafter the anesthesia service began in-house coverage at the attending level, and dedicated, highly skilled teams for pediatric and cardiac anesthesia were developed.

The involvement of the anesthesia service in the management of critically ill patients increased, and our role gradually diminished, as the number of ICU beds expanded. Anesthesia came to play a larger role in the recovery room, which had previously been the exclusive domain of the surgical residents.

Part of the role of the middle and senior residents was to teach medical students and junior house officers. Some of this teaching took place during shared on-duty time in the evenings and nights. Some took place in the operating room, where almost all procedures involved a senior or chief resident helping a more junior resident with a procedure.

An extra one or two years' experience came into play and affected the quality of the teaching. The majority of senior and chief residents had interrupted their training after two or three years to serve in the military or at the NIH, where two of the five coveted positions at the heart or cancer institute seemed to be reserved for the MGH residents.

The east and west services were our home base, where we worked with our colleagues. The middle and senior residents had a chance to teach to interns, junior residents, and medical students. They in turn exercised senior responsibility in the operating room and were mentored by the chief residents and, when asked, by the visiting staff.

CHAPTER 8:   VASCULAR

"You gotta do it right, boy."

-- Dr. Robert R. Linton

My own interest as I progressed through the residency was in vascular surgery, in which the MGH was exceptionally strong. Dr. Robert Linton was the senior vascular surgeon at the MGH and one of the pioneer vascular surgeons in the United States as well.

Dr. Linton was known as "Linto," but the house staff always addressed him as Dr. Linton. He was also known as the "GBE"—the Great Bald Eagle—having developed *alopecia totalis* in the 1920s, making him an even more formidable and unusual personage. In his youth, he had climbed mountains and been a college pole vaulter. In later years, he was an avid skier and sailor.

In 1931, he was appointed chief of the vascular clinic by Dr. Arthur Allen. At that time, arterial surgery was far in the future, and even venous surgery had a significant morbidity, primarily due to infections. Dr. Linton made his initial reputation as a venous surgeon, writing seminal papers that defined the importance of the communicating veins in venous insufficiency and their contribution to venous ulcers.

The Aesculapiad, Harvard Medical School's yearbook, predicted in 1940 that "the sun will still be shining on Bob Linton's bald head when the Peter Bent Brigham bites the dust." Nearly forty years later, when the Brigham was demolished to be replaced by a new facility and merged with the Boston Lying-In Hospital, readers of the yearbook were reminded of this prediction.

The operation he later championed became known as the Linton Procedure. It was a radical operation involving excision of both the lesser and greater saphenous veins along with the communicating veins and the venous ulcer, combined with applying a split-thickness skin graft to the ulcer bed. Later, what was commonly performed under this rubric was a modification of the original operation and consisted of subfascial ligation of the communicating veins through a median calf incision along with excision and skin grafting of the venous ulcer.

This operation was unforgiving of technical errors and is almost never performed today, as it has been supplanted by simpler and less invasive interventions.

Dr. Linton ultimately became a champion of femoral popliteal bypass grafts for arterial occlusive disease in the 1950s and 1960s, although he had been rather slow to accept the validity and durability of this procedure.

I had spent time in France as a medical student and had come to know Dr. Jean Kunlin of Paris. Although he was a generation older than I, we became friends, and I was a guest at his home in Paris on several occasions. Kunlin had performed the first reversed saphenous vein graft for occlusive disease in the late 1940s while his mentor, Professor Rene Leriche, was on vacation.

Because he had not trained in Paris, French medical politics prevented Leriche from having his own service at any of the prestigious Paris hospitals. Jean Kunlin operated at the American Hospital in Neuilly. After retirement he returned to the investigative laboratory. I was able to help him obtain honorary membership in the Society for Vascular Surgery, whose membership at the time was limited to 220 surgeons in North America. In 1990 he wrote to me, "My wife and I are becoming old". I was saddened to learn of his passing less than two years later.

Kunlin's original technique had been to construct an end-to-side anastomosis with the saphenous vein to the host artery, opening the artery longitudinally, thus allowing the anastomosis to be beveled (*anastomose elargissante*) to maximize flow. Dr. Linton originally divided both the femoral and popliteal arteries completely, constructing an end-to-end anastomosis, but eventually adopted Dr.Kunlin's technique.

Dr. Linton had a characteristic speech pattern, with an exhalation-grunt at the end of a sentence, which Kunlin convincingly imitated. As he recounted to me, Dr. Linton asked him how many grafts had occluded postop.

"Not as many as you think."

"In Boston, our patency rate is very high."

"But how can you be sure they remain open if you don't do postop arteriograms?"

Then ensued a debate between Dr. Linton and Jean Kunlin about the need for postop arteriograms, which Dr. Kunlin advocated as part of the follow-up.

Before grafts were available for aortic aneurysm repair, he introduced long wires into the aneurysm sac, causing it to partially thrombose, thus preventing further aneurysm expansion and rupture.

Dr. Linton was a meticulous technician, whose trademark expression was, "Do it right, boy!" All the residents were addressed as boy. If there was any bleeding from an arterial anastomosis, he would reclamp the artery and put in one remedial stitch. If this was insufficient, he would reclamp, take the entire anastomosis down and redo it. Sometimes he redid an anastomosis several times before he was satisfied.

One of the residents was helping with an arterial bypass, and Dr. Linton looked at the finished anastomosis and said, "What do you think, John?"

Now, a resident is very hesitant to criticize a senior surgeon's technical work, and Dr. Linton interpreted a split second of the resident's hesitation as he wished. Before the resident could answer, Dr. Linton concluded, "That's no damn good." Clamps reapplied to artery, sutures removed, anastomosis redone.

Dr. Linton pioneered the use of splenorenal shunts for the treatment of esophageal varices and modified the Sengstaken-Blakemore tube used for emergency control of massive variceal bleeding. The Linton tube had a large gastric balloon that was filled with 700 cc of air and then placed on traction with a one-kilogram weight attached to a pulley that passed over the foot of the bed to tamponade the bleeding varices.

He was one of the founding members of the Society for Vascular Surgery, and his presidential address in 1955 was the first to deal with arterial reconstruction.

When I worked with him as a resident, he was seventy years old and had become set in his ways. He had not changed some of his techniques, which had been supplanted by newer, simpler, and quicker approaches.

What Dr. Linton taught so successfully to several decades of surgical residents was the gentle, meticulous handling of blood vessels, and the mindset to insist on a rigorous self-discipline in the OR that did not allow acceptance of anything less than technical perfection. He included a sketch of the operation performed in his operative note for clarity—a little extra touch that most of us who rotated on his service thereafter followed.

At the time, there were very few vascular surgeons in New England experienced in arterial reconstructions, and Dr. Linton had a large following. He was much harsher with patients than would be considered acceptable today, as many of them believed, probably correctly, that there were few other surgeons available with comparable expertise. Hence not much chance for a second opinion.

Dr. Linton insisted that patients stop smoking and achieve an acceptable body weight prior to operation. His not infrequent comment to patients was, "You're too goddamn fat!" He would then send the patient home with instructions to lose the requisite amount of weight and then have them telephone his office to schedule an elective procedure.

One weekend, when I was in the private vascular service, a patient had been admitted Sunday afternoon and had complained that Dr. Linton had not come in to see him. When told of this on rounds the next morning, he grunted, walked into the room, and commanded the patient to "Get on the scale!"

The reading was one or two pounds above the recommended weight, and Dr. Linton simply said, "You're still too goddamn fat. Go home and lose more weight before you come back." Such communication would not be tolerated today.

If the circulating nurse was not in the operating room when he needed her, Dr. Linton would pick up the large saline-filled basin used to rinse powder from surgeons' gloves and heave it into the corridor. Guaranteed to get attention.

He had other, equally memorable traits and idiosyncrasies. He wore a gold OR cap with one star on it (because there can only be one star …). He used linen thread for ligatures, which he cut with a sharpened Keith needle. After harvesting the saphenous vein for a bypass, he ran a fine silk suture along its length to prevent twisting after doing the anastomosis. He did a two-layer anastomosis of aorta to graft. Took longer, but never leaked.

Prior to clamping the aorta, he insisted on injecting the heparin himself into the inferior vena cava, explaining that he had once operated on a Vermont farmer who was now "six feet under the ground" because the "anesthesia boy" had forgotten to give the heparin when asked to do so.

Long before I was a resident, Dr. Linton had operated on Bob Hope's brother. Dr. Linton and Bob Hope were coming up the elevator together to visit, and one of the Phillips House nurses was overheard telling her colleague "I just saw Bob Hope and Yul Brynner coming off the elevator!"

One of the last true Linton legends was the resection of a thoraco-abdominal aneurysm, requiring a left subclavian artery to bilateral femoral artery bypass with grafts to all visceral vessels: 13 anastomoses, a gastrostomy, seven scrub nurses, five anesthesiologists, and three surgical residents, one of whom developed superficial phlebitis after the operation. The operation lasted twenty-three hours. Dr. Linton was seventy years old at the time.

Dr. Linton devised knee-length support stockings—called Linton stockings of course—to treat the edema associated with chronic venous insufficiency. He had them manufactured by Trueform in Cincinnati. I do not think he ever realized a meaningful profit, but part of his arrangement was that each house officer received a pair annually without charge. They had rubber woven into the weave, were hot and much less comfortable than the lighter garments available today, but they were invaluable for house officers required to stand in the OR all day.

Dr. Linton worked for several decades on his *Atlas of Vascular Surgery*, finally published in 1973 by W.B. Saunders. It was 499 pages long, with text on the left side of the page and illustrations on the right. It contains much of the basics he taught for so long, pictures of the instruments he used, and innumerable pieces of technical advice.

Dr. Linton had been seriously hurt in an auto accident in Maine on a July Fourth weekend. He was transported by ambulance to the MGH and found to have multiple fractures, a ruptured spleen, and a torn small bowel mesentery. What had not been known was that long-term steroid use for his asthma had rendered him diabetic. He had a tempestuous course in the ICU requiring a tracheostomy and prolonged ventilator support. His life was probably saved on several occasions by the resident staff.

When I returned from the Army on October 1 for my senior resident year, he had just been transferred out of the ICU. The resident I replaced told me, "We pulled Dr. Linton through a number of times. Everyone was afraid of him dying on his night on and being forever labeled as the resident who let Dr. Linton die. Don't you be the one." Welcome back to the MGH.

Dr. Linton eventually recovered and was able to return to his office, but did not operate again. He passed away in 1979.

My principal teacher in vascular surgery was the late Dr. R. Clement Darling. Dr. Darling had been a marine in World War II, attended medical school, and graduated first in his class from Boston University. He was the first graduate of Boston University's medical school to be accepted for the MGH surgical program.

Clem was an exceptionally talented technician and spent time with Drs. Michael DeBakey and E. Stanley Crawford in Houston before returning to the MGH as a staff surgeon, where he worked as Dr. Linton's assistant for a number of years after returning.

Clem was always available to help and advise the residents, and was very generous with his time. He was temperamental and generated more than his share of memorable quotes. For instance, he once described using a bovine graft sewn to a tibial artery as "sewing an elephant's trunk to a mouse's urethra."

Clem was angered by patients who continued to smoke as only reformed smokers are. One morning on rounds, he came upon a patient on whom he had struggled for five or six hours the previous day to construct a complicated tibial graft. When he entered the room, the patient was sitting in bed smoking a cigarette causing Clem to become red in the face. He crushed the cigarette out in the ashtray and, to be sure it was definitively extinguished, emptied the patient's bedside urinal into the ashtray.

Dr. R. Clement Darling, Jr. (Courtesy
of Dr. R. Clement Darling, III)

Clem helped me with my first carotid endarterectomy as a senior resident. A carotid endarterectomy was one of the key operations that senior residents look forward to doing for the first time.

The customary procedure was for the vascular fellow to assist the resident in dissecting out the vessels and getting ready to heparinize and cross clamp, then to page Dr. Darling to come to the operating room and assist with the crucial part of the operation.

Dr. David Brewster, later one of the more preeminent vascular surgeons in the United States was the fellow when I was a resident. Dr. Darling's long-term scrub nurse, Carlene Messina, was scrubbed. She was an invaluable teacher who helped train innumerable residents by graciously and silently giving the resident the correct instrument at the right time.

I dissected out the common, internal, and external carotid vessels and was ready to heparinize and clamp these vessels. We paged Dr. Darling, who didn't answer. We paged him again, and still no answer. Dave Brewster said to go ahead and clamp and do it.

"What? Before Dr. Darling gets here?"

"That is what he wants you to do."

Carlene agreed. I was outvoted. So with more than the usual trepidation when performing a major operation for the first time, I heparinized, cross clamped, opened the artery, put the shunt in, cleaned the artery out, and then got it closed when Clem Darling arrived in the operating room.

"Why the hell didn't you page me?"

Dave Brewster said, "We did, Dr. Darling." I agreed. So did Carlene.

"I never got the page. If he strokes it will be your goddamn fault."

Great encouragement. With that exit line, he left the operating room. That was my first carotid endarterectomy. Dr. Churchill had said that a surgeon who doesn't wake up at 2:00 a.m. and worry about his patients shouldn't be operating. I worried about the patient for the next three days, checking on him several times a day. Fortunately, he did well and was discharged without any neurologic deficit.

Clem was often mercurial, usually outspoken, and politically incorrect before the term was invented. I liked him instantly. When I returned to the MGH for my last year of residency and introduced my new bride, Clem's comment was, "Are you the same one as last year?"

"Clem, are you trying to get me in major trouble at home?"

"Hell, you guys change women all the time. How am I supposed to keep up?"

Clem published a series of over five hundred patients with abdominal aneurysms in the 1970s with a mortality rate of 1.7 percent—an extraordinary success rate in a time prior to today's more advanced interventional cardiology, treatment of coronary artery disease, and critical care medicine.

One of Clem's major accomplishments, for which he never received much credit, was his role in the development of the noninvasive vascular laboratory. Dr. Jeff Raines, an MIT graduate student, had developed a plethysmograph called the PVR (pulse volume recorder) to measure arterial wave forms and obtain pressures at various points in the extremity. It eventually proved to be a valuable addition to the vascular surgery armamentarium, although many of the senior vascular surgeons in the United States were skeptical that this would add much to their clinical skills.

Clem and David Brewster allowed Jeff to study many of the vascular patients pre- and postop, including in the recovery room. The senior residents helped. The results of five thousand clinical exams were presented to the Society for Vascular Surgery in 1971, and the MGH vascular lab influenced the initiation of vascular laboratories in nearly all hospitals. The PVR technology and its successors are now routinely used for arterial evaluation, and vascular laboratories now also study carotid vessels and the venous system with ultrasound. The MGH Vascular Lab as of 2011 had seventeen full-time employees and performed fourteen thousand examinations annually.

Clem became a *de facto* godfather for the MGH residents going into vascular surgery, many of whom became heads of divisions of vascular surgery at major institutions—Cincinnati, U Mass, Emory, Ohio State, Johns Hopkins, and Tufts. Later, I coauthored a couple of papers with him, and he and David Brewster contributed a chapter to a small book I edited. After I left the MGH, he was most gracious in helping follow some unusual patients I had operated on and sponsored me for membership in the national vascular societies. He certainly was one of the major influences on my training and career, for which I remain grateful.

CHAPTER 9:   CARDIAC

One doughnut only

Cardiac surgery and cardiopulmonary bypass are now quite routine and not limited to large academic medical centers. Such was not always the case.

Four years prior to rotating as a junior resident on the cardiac surgery service, I was a third-year medical student on my surgical rotation, the first clinical rotation of my third year. My recollections of cardiac operations were of exceptionally long preparation in the OR involving saphenous vein cutdowns for intravenous access, long operations, and a high complication and mortality rate. I wondered if I should rethink my plan to apply for a surgical internship, but I did not.

Dr. John Gibbon worked in Dr. Churchill's research laboratory at the MGH starting in 1934 and ultimately performed the first intracardiac repair under cardiopulmonary bypass in Philadelphia in 1953. In 1956, the first successful open-heart operation with cardiopulmonary bypass was performed at the MGH for an atrial septal defect. If a single person could be credited with the development of cardiac surgery at the MGH, it would be Dr. W. Gerald Austen. Dr. Austen was a visiting cardiac surgeon when I began internship and about two years later was named as surgery department chairman.

In the mid-1950s, Dr. Austen, then a Harvard medical student and an MIT graduate with mechanical engineering expertise, was put on a team charged with building a heart-lung machine by Drs. Gordon Scannell and Robert Shaw. The problems, which were eventually overcome, included preventing damage to red blood cells by the perfusion equipment, and prevention of clotting of the blood in the machine. The former could cause kidney damage from free hemoglobin; blood clotting while on cardiopulmonary bypass can cause stroke and major organ injury.

Dr. W. Gerald (Jerry) Austen at work early in his MGH career. (Courtesy of the Massachusetts General Hospital)

Jerry Austen was one of a number of individuals at the Mass General who could survive on minimum sleep and who performed significant investigative work while working as resident, despite being on duty every other night in the hospital. On his nights off, he worked in the White Building basement and in the basement and garage of Robert Shaw's house. They paid their own expenses for equipment.

As a resident, he was sent to England and worked at King's College Hospital in London and in Leeds. By the end of residency, he had accumulated fifteen scientific publications and was named as chief resident after only four and a half years of the residency.

He returned to Boston after two years at the NIH Heart Institute and advanced from instructor to tenured associate professor two years later, at age thirty-six, and then to chairman of the department of surgery a couple years later. He helped develop the intra-aortic balloon pump—which was lifesaving for many individuals in cardiogenic shock from heart disease—and studied the effects of controlled coronary perfusion and the acute effects of ventricular aneurysms.

Heart surgery developed very rapidly at the MGH as Dr. Austen recruited three successive chief residents to join him on the cardiac service: Mortimer Buckley, Eldred Mundth, and Willard Daggett. The mortality for cardiac surgery in 1958 was 25%; when I was a junior resident on the service, it was 14%; by 2000, it was 2.7%, including emergencies.

Ultimately, Dr. Austen was author or coauthor of more than four hundred publications, fifty-one book chapters, and four textbooks. He was the first surgeon to be president of the American Heart Association and was president of seven other societies as well. Dr. Roman DeSanctis, director emeritus of clinical cardiology, said, "Dr. Jerry Austen is the most important physician—really the most important person—to work at the MGH in the last fifty years, and in fact, one of the most important physicians in the two-hundred-year history of this institution."

During my residency, most open-heart operations in adults were done for valvular heart disease secondary to rheumatic fever and streptococcal infections decades earlier. At that time, these patients were usually operated on in the late stages of the natural history of their disease, when they had developed significant pulmonary impairment from pulmonary hypertension.

The cardiac surgery rotation was one of the most grueling for the surgical residents, although the lessons learned regarding care of critically ill patients, ventilator management, and operative technique were invaluable. There were no intensivists, and although the cardiologists were helpful, the residents became comfortable dealing with coagulation problems, cardiac arrhythmias, and complicated fluid and electrolyte problems in patients with sick hearts, lungs, and kidneys.

Four junior residents and two senior residents covered the cardiac service, which had its own dedicated ICU several years before a general surgery ICU was created. The junior resident would spend every other day in the operating room, where he would be responsible for exposing the femoral artery for cannulation and then repairing the artery at the end of the procedure. This was an important technical skill that we would later apply to major peripheral vascular operations as senior residents. On the alternate days, he would remain in the cardiac ICU and be charged with the care of the postoperative cardiac surgery patients.

The surgical house staff were not superstitious, but we were often ritualistic. Certain rituals were undertaken tongue in cheek, like wearing a certain hat in the OR for difficult cases. Thus evolved the "sham closure" on the cardiac service, which was employed when I was the cardiac junior resident, though it apparently began about a decade earlier.

A surgeon who needs to reexplore his patient for postoperative bleeding always expresses incredulity and argues, "It was dry when I closed." Cardiopulmonary bypass mandates high doses of heparin to prevent the patient's blood from clotting, much higher doses than we use for peripheral vascular surgery. Before closing the chest, hemostasis (normal blood clotting) must be restored, otherwise the patient will bleed after operation, potentially causing a life-threatening complication (cardiac tamponade) or a wound hematoma requiring reexploration.

After the visiting cardiac surgeon left the room, the resident team was charged with "drying up" and closing the sternotomy. Someone personified the capillaries and small vessels, saying that they fiendishly conspired to wait until the wound was closed and bleeding not visible to the operating team. Only then did they begin bleeding, thereby requiring the patient to be returned to the OR, and obligating the resident to report this complication at the weekly conference.

After generous use of cautery, wound packing, and combinations of Gelfoam, Surgicel and topical thrombin, the OR lights were turned off, the residents waited on either side of the OR table with hemostats in hand, uttering loud exclamations like "Sure is dark in here!" or "What a neat skin closure!," designed to trick the small wound vessels into bleeding. A pregnant pause ensued, after which the lights were turned on, the packing removed, and attempts at hemostasis resumed.

The only glitch was that the open-heart operations were done in one of the White Building ORs with a viewing gallery and intercom system on the floor above, enabling two-way communications and direct visualization of the OR. One of the chiefs was escorting some visiting overseas surgeons, saw that the lights were out but that the residents were loudly talking.

"What the hell is going on down there?"

"We're working on the sham closure—almost have the oozing controlled." Technique subsequently abandoned.

Our work schedule posed several practical problems for the resident. One was fatigue, which was inescapable since we are often up every one to two hours during the night attending to abrupt changes in patients' status. The other problem was that of nutrition.

The junior resident spent every other day in the operating room as second assistant, and the intervening days either on the postop cardiac surgery floor or in the intensive care unit. He was not allowed to leave the ICU except for morning rounds. The patients in the ICU, both adult and pediatric, required very close care with frequent attention to respiratory difficulties, ventilators, pressors to control blood pressure, electrolyte balance, and blood replacement.

If you could not leave the ICU, you depended on the other junior resident either to relieve you for thirty minutes in the late evening to partake of the free hospital meal for on-duty house staff or to bring a meal to the cardiac ICU. If the other resident was tied up, you did not get to eat from breakfast to breakfast.

The very nice amenity provided by Dr. Austen was what we called the "cardiac doughnuts." Each day, Hawkins, an OR aide recruited from the NIH, would bring in a dozen doughnuts. There was an obvious honor system, since there were just enough donuts for the staff surgeons, residents, and Hawkins. It was dishonorable to have more than one doughnut, no matter how hungry you might be.

The other unwritten law was that you were not allowed to take the yellow-custard-filled doughnut—Dr. Austen's favorite. We identified the flavor of the filled doughnuts by probing them with a wooden tongue blade, and the residents quickly deemed Dr. Austen's favorite as the "yellow pus-pockets." Once told this, Jerry Austen remarked that he might not be able to eat one ever again.

Even with a doughnut in the morning, one might be obligated to go a full twenty-four hours without a meal. We often solved this problem by ordering high-protein diets on some of the patients in the ICU, which usually involved steak. Since most of the patients in the unit were on ventilators and unable to eat, an occasional overzealous dietitian would come by and demand an explanation about how a patient with an endotracheal tube in place on a ventilator could eat.

"We usually take the tube out at meal time and then replace it afterwards," was the explanation.

Some of the dietitians seemed confused; others realized that the residents were consuming the meals and walked off smiling. A few years later, a meal tray would appear for the ICU junior resident, courtesy of the senior surgical staff.

Dr. Austen was always cognizant of the residents' enormous workload, particularly on the cardiac service. Occasionally, on the postoperative cardiac floor, he would come by and offer to take care of the daily anticoagulation orders for the resident on duty. The trick was to have the orders written before Jerry arrived so as not to lose face by letting the chief do the resident's work.

Coronary bypass surgery was begun at the MGH when I was a resident, and over the ensuing decade, it supplanted valvular heart disease for rheumatic valve problems on the operative list. Bill Daggett and Mort Buckley developed expertise in operating on children with congenital heart disease, and pediatric heart surgery likewise became a major part of our workload.

Cardiac transplantation was eventually begun after considerable disagreement on the part of the medical staff and the trustees about whether the hospital should undertake this much of a commitment and devote the necessary resources to make it outstanding. Over the ensuing years, the cardiac service, now a division, has continued to develop its armamentarium. There are currently seven staff cardiothoracic surgeons, and 1,300 operations are done each year. Individual staff members have specific expertise in mechanical circulatory support, minimally invasive valve surgery, and the management of pulmonary emboli. Team effort is stressed, as is maximal efficiency in OR scheduling.

The cardiac surgeons I worked with are no longer operating. Dr. Thoraf Sundt III, an MGH trainee, returned to head the division of cardiac surgery. The training program is able to take general surgery residents from within our own program, who spend four years in general surgery and then three years in the cardiothoracic training program. Three residents are taken each year, one in cardiac and two in thoracic surgery.

CHAPTER 10: HIATUS

After four years working every other night, I was ready for a break in my training. We had a succession of Dutch surgical residents who spent a year in the research labs and then as residents for six to twelve months on the private service where they did very little operating but were exposed to the senior MGH surgeons. These residents were all smart, hard-working, and personable.

I spoke with Dr. George Nardi about taking a year off to work in Europe, and through one of his previous research fellows, he was able to arrange a position for me as a resident at the Sint Lucas Ziekenhuis in Amsterdam, affiliated with the Free University. I arrived in Amsterdam the first week of July and was met by one of the chief residents at Schiphol airport.

Housing was very difficult to come by in Amsterdam and required a lengthy wait. Sint Lucas arranged for me to have a small apartment behind the hospital, between the student nurses' dorm and the hospital priest's apartment, about 100 yards from the front entrance. I bought a couple of items of furniture, a half refrigerator, and two hotplates, but had most of my meals in the hospital cafeteria.

The Dutch surgical training system was very different from ours. First, it was not a fixed program for a specific number of years. A resident advanced in seniority as older residents moved on and remained in training until his chief thought he was fully trained and ready to seek a staff position. At the time, there was no board examination, as we had in the United States. The chief resident usually spent three or four years at this level until he found an appropriate staff position, similar to the senior registrars in the United Kingdom.

The result was that a chief resident was very well trained, capable of operating without supervision, and comparable to a junior attending surgeon in the United States. He rotated call with the attending surgeons, a very good deal for the hospital as chief residents were paid at a much lower level than the attending surgeons.

I found that I was very well prepared in terms of patient management, because the junior house staff in Amsterdam did not have nearly the responsibility or experience we had in Boston. The only significant gap in my preparation was in fracture management, including open reductions and internal fixation, which at the time was done by general surgeons in Holland. I had had no experience with fractures in Boston.

"How can you be a general and trauma surgeon if you cannot do fractures?" I was asked.

"How can you do fractures if you are not able to handle late complications, such as aseptic necrosis of the hip after open reduction of a hip fracture?"

The real answer was that there were not enough orthopedic surgeons in Holland, and they were certainly not willing to take emergency call. I nevertheless felt somewhat uncomfortable at the chief resident level having to call a more junior resident for advice on fractures.

The training in Amsterdam was serious, and standards were high, but there was less formality and regimentation than at the MGH. We had all of our patients on one floor, made morning rounds as a group with the head nurse, then trooped down to the cafeteria for coffee before going to the operating room. There was a daily 1:00 p.m. conference to discuss pending operations, and a quick meeting late in the afternoon to discuss the day's operations and sick patients. Everyone smoked during these conferences, and I became somewhat addicted to small Dutch cigars.

The turnover time between operations was short, in large measure because anesthesia was different than in the United States because of minimal AFAT (anesthesia fooling around time). It was casual enough to frighten me during major cases. The patient would be given Halothane—a vasodilating inhalational agent, and only after induction would a peripheral IV be started. Central lines were almost never used. I once asked for one for an abdominal aneurysm repair and the anesthesiologist said, "What for?"

We almost always finished our elective cases by 1:00 p.m. At 11:30, a big tureen of soup and a tray of sandwiches were brought to the operating room for the staff who were still working. A very gracious tradition was that a resident doing an operation for the first time brought pastries for the OR the following day.

The night call was much more relaxed than I was used to, generally about every third or fourth night. There were far fewer complicated, critically ill patients than in Boston. There was a refrigerator stocked with Coca Cola and Heineken beer in the residents' lounge for the resident on duty at night.

Since I lived on the hospital grounds and was close by, if any acute problems arose, the residents would say, "Call Jarrett, he's used to working every other night anyway and he won't mind."

There were far fewer instruments in the operating room than in Boston, where the number of instruments available for a simple procedure under local anesthesia were enough for a thoracotomy. I learned to do with less. Packaged sutures with swedged-on needles were only available for specific circumstances, such as vascular reconstructions. The necessary sutures were stored in bulk in the OR as spools in large sterile containers. The circulating nurse would grab the end of one with a sterile instrument, cut it to the appropriate length, and pass it onto the sterile operating field where the surgeon would load it onto a needle.

Work grounds were likewise very different. There were almost no written orders. The head nurse made rounds with the residents, pushing the dressing cart. The nurses removed drains, chest tubes, and sutures. The first time I tried to write orders I was immediately chastised by the head nurse.

"We cannot be expected to read all the doctors' handwritings. Just tell me what you want, and we will get it done." She was correct.

We had fixed orders for most situations—activity, diet, lab work. Once the patients could eat, the nurses advanced the diet as they saw fit. Patients were generally healthy, accustomed to exercise, noncomplaining, and did very well. Meals were never served in the patient's bed. There was a small table in each four-bed room, and at mealtime, the patients would go from bed to table and take their meal, promoting early ambulation.

Everyone was multilingual and could jump effortlessly from English to Dutch. The secretarial staff was so good that one could dictate in Dutch, English, German, or French and expect to have a flawless note returned.

I could not speak a word of Dutch when I arrived, and the other residents did not think this would be a problem. One of the chief residents was from the Philippines and spoke only rudimentary Dutch after seven years. The interns and junior residents dictated her operative notes and discharge letters.

The other residents opined that it would be impossible for me to learn Dutch. I considered this a challenge. The gauntlet had been thrown.

With nothing much to do most evenings, I would come to the hospital and study the typewritten portions of the chart—operative notes and discharge summaries. The student nurses brought me coffee. With a dictionary in hand, I managed to learn medical Dutch within a couple of months.

My first operation caused a great deal of laughter among the other residents: not the operation itself, but dictating the operative note, which drew a small audience. Initially, I often had to ask someone for a correct medical term or description, but vowed to dictate all my operative notes and discharge summaries in Dutch, and I did for the entire year.

I learned a great deal in Amsterdam. First, I gained additional experience in examining patients. I realized that at the MGH, I had never examined a patient with an acute abdomen with a senior surgeon. The continental surgeons were expert at physical diagnosis and depended less on laboratory tests and X-rays.

I learned a number of new techniques. I did a great deal of hepato-biliary and gastric surgery. We had a standard procedure for performing gastrectomies, using a Shoemaker clamp. I became quite comfortable with this, although the identical instrumentation was not available when I returned to Boston.

In return, I was able to introduce a couple of operations and techniques to Sint Lucas that I had learned in Boston, which were well accepted. One was total parenteral nutrition through a central intravenous line, which we had just started in Boston but was new in the Netherlands.

I spent my first two months as a senior resident running the working emergency room and then was promoted to chief resident.

The only impairment was that my wife-to-be, a Canadian immunologist whom I had met while sailing the prior November, was not with me. I convinced her to pass up a position at the Scripps Clinic in San Diego to relocate from Vancouver to Boston in the middle of a New England winter.

I was on duty at the MGH every other night, chronically fatigued on my nights off, not well-paid, relocating six months later, and committed to the Army for two years afterward. Why did she come? Inexplicable, but nevertheless one of the great diplomatic coups of the twentieth century.

However, bureaucracy was alive and well then as it is now. Esther's visa was held up for several months because the Royal Canadian Mounted Police had to certify her lack of a criminal record before the U.S. consulate would issue a visa.

I communicated with the consulate on several occasions, saying that I was calling from the MGH in Boston. My senator's staff made polite but persistent inquiries. My wife's future supervisor at Children's Hospital wrote that children were dying because Esther was not in Boston to do preoperative tissue typing for their kidney transplants.

When Esther was finally given her visa, the consular official made her promise to get everyone off his back and added, "I'm not sure what's such a big deal about being able to type on tissue paper."

With her credentials, Esther was offered a position half a year later at the TNO in Rijswijk, the Dutch equivalent of the NIH. She arrived in September and found an apartment in Delft. The Friday after she arrived, we arranged to have a celebratory dinner at the Prinsenkelder, an elegant restaurant on a canal in central Amsterdam.

Courtship does not always go as planned. That afternoon, I had evaluated a patient with chronic ulcer disease and an ulcer perforation. I had just finished reviewing the MGH experience with perforated ulcers, where we advocated a gastrectomy in the setting of chronicity, which this patient had.

I was eager to perform my first gastrectomy in Holland. Although I was not on call that evening, I scheduled the patient, and we started the operation late in the afternoon.

Esther arrived to meet me at the restaurant, but I was still in the operating room. Cellphones did not yet exist. We did not carry pagers. When I did not arrive, she prevailed upon the restaurant to call the hospital. The hospital operator insisted I was not there.

The operator knew who was on call, and only the persons on call were in the hospital after hours on a Friday evening. This was Europe. "He's not here!"

After another half hour or so, Esther had the restaurant call the hospital again. The telephone operator became somewhat irate: "Why would he be here? He does not have *dienst*. He is obviously not here. I cannot look for him."

When I finally finished the gastrectomy, I telephoned the restaurant with my still rudimentary Dutch language skills, "Do you speak English?" I asked somewhat apologetically.

"Is your name Jarrett? If it is, there is a very attractive young lady down here who is being offered drinks and dinner by half the men in the restaurant. I suggest you get your butt down here very quickly because if you don't, she won't be here when you arrive."

That was our first dinner in Amsterdam.

We had a great year in Holland. We could drive to Belgium or France on a weekend and fly to London on student airfares in time to go the theater Friday evening. We were married in Vancouver the following June.

At Sint Lucas, all patients were anticoagulated postoperatively with a coumadin derivative. The MGH had a long-standing interest in postoperative venous thrombosis and, for a time, did routine prophylactic superficial femoral vein ligations after major operations. But we had been accustomed to only anticoagulating persons at high risk or those with documented thromboembolic disease.

I asked, "What about the routine hernias, gallbladders,and sympathectomies?"

"We anticoagulate everyone."

"Do you have many wound hematomas or bleeding?"

"Very few. We place suction drains at the end of the operation in most of the patients and remove them at forty-eight hours."

I feared having a large number of patients with postoperative bleeding or hematomas, but my fears were not realized. I placed drains for elective operations that I was used to closing without drainage. To my surprise, we saw almost no thromboembolic complications and very few wound hematomas in my year as chief resident. Postoperative thromboembolic prophylaxis is now pretty much routine in the United States for most operations, so the Dutch were several decades ahead of us.

There was a dedicated system of visiting nurses—the *trombosedienst,* who visited the patients at home twice a week, checked the prothrombin times and reported back to our service. We could then adjust the dose of anticoagulation given if needed by using a check sheet.

A weekly M & M (morbidity and mortality) conference was held, just as in American teaching hospitals. One of the residents asked me, "What do you do in Boston if your chief has a death or complication?"

"We discuss it candidly just as any other problem." He seemed incredulous.

At the end of the year, the chief of surgery proposed me for membership in the Dutch Surgical Society, which I have continued over the ensuing decades and found to be a rewarding experience and a way to keep in touch with former colleagues and friends.

When I eventually returned to the MGH, we continued to have one or two Dutch residents working in the research lab and on the house staff. Most of these became close friends. At one juncture, the surgery department chairmen at four of the eight Dutch medical schools were alumni of the MGH research lab and residency experience.

After a very busy and productive year in Holland, we returned to the United States, where I entered the Army for a two-year commitment. My initial assignment was to Korea, preceded by a month at Fort Sam Houston, Texas, for training. We had a very relaxing month with no night call for the first time in five years, and a more generous salary than I was used to. Esther helped set up a tissue typing program at a lab in San Antonio during our month there. Her only trouble was that she had difficulty understanding the Texas drawl.

I spent two years in the Army, the first as a surgeon at the 121st Evacuation Hospital in Seoul, the second as chief of surgery at the army hospital at Ft. Meade, Maryland. Technically, I was not board eligible because I had not done my last year of residency in an approved American training program, but I felt quite comfortable technically, having done a very large volume of operative surgery in Holland and worked at the chief resident level.

I was asked to serve as consultant in general surgery for U.S./ U.N. forces Korea. In wartime, this position was usually filled by someone of professorial status, but in reality, we saw very little major trauma. My major role was to visit smaller medical facilities without inpatient capabilities and advise the medical officers on surgical issues. I also talked my way into an appointment as a lecturer at Seoul National University Hospital, where I made a weekly visit to lecture or make rounds.

Korea was considered a "hardship tour." It was not really a hardship by any means, and the pace of work was leisurely compared to Amsterdam and vacation-like compared to the MGH. Esther was able to join me about a month after I arrived, and we had an excellent and productive year in Korea.

I found that the opportunity to work with surgeons trained in other good programs was a learning experience. When I returned to the MGH, I felt very comfortable with my operative experience in general surgery, but I had not done much vascular surgery in Holland and almost none in the Army.

But reentry was somewhat difficult. I was back in a white suit after spending thirty-eight months away from Boston, almost as long as my four initial years as an MGH resident . I had been chief resident for a year in Holland, a staff surgeon for two years in the Army, where the most senior surgeon was only a year or two older and had done more gastrectomies and trauma surgery than any of the other senior residents.

It was a difficult readjustment for some of the services where I was the only resident, being called to do admission histories and physicals and some of the ubiquitous scut work. One of the senior surgeons had opined, "You're always an intern at the MGH."

I knew only a minority of the residents I was working with, and some of the other senior residents had been interns when I left. I was willing to help the junior residents with a number of major procedures that I had done a large volume of while away—gastric resections and major biliary tract surgery—which the other senior residents felt obligated to do themselves.

Before the year finished, I passed the qualifying exam for fellowship designation by the Royal College of Surgeons of Canada, who counted my chief year in Holland as the required senior training. For the American Board of Surgery, I had to finish my senior year at the MGH before taking the exam.

I tried to apply some of what I had learned while away. But all of the senior staff were MGH trained, and things changed very, very slowly. For example, only one or two surgeons had begun using staplers because the most senior GI surgeons were not convinced that the technique would be durable.

Limited operations for breast cancer were adopted reluctantly, and at first, a couple of the residents thought that anything less than a total mastectomy was unethical and refused to assist the senior surgeon who advocated lesser procedures.

I did a couple of gastrectomies with a Billroth I reconstruction rather than the Billroth II (attaching the stomach remnant to the duodenum—gastroduodenostomy—rather than to the upper small intestine—gastrojejunostomy) practiced by all the senior staff. Such produced some harsh criticism from the senior staff. If they could have court-martialed or pilloried me, they would have. But I still think the former is more physiologic and has a lower complication rate.

What had I learned while away?

Not only was there more than one way to do an operation, but probably two or three. I worked with able, well-trained surgeons in the Army, and we benefited from exposure to each other's training. I felt that, despite the unequaled dedication to patient care and the tradition of excellence, the MGH would have been well served by some new blood. Such was gradually accomplished over the ensuing years.

The workload was not as arduous as it was before I left. If Sundays were quiet, Esther would come to the surgeons' lounge with a picnic lunch and our newborn in a stroller. Usually we had time to finish our lunch between interruptions. For the first time, I realized that, nearly eight years after I had started, an end to my training was in sight.

CHAPTER 11: THEN AND NOW

The internship examination still exists, and remains challenging. The intellectual bastinado of the past has been tempered, and the examination is more civilized. The MGH Department of Surgery currently receives more than six hundred applications from the United States for first-year positions and an equal number from foreign applicants. Eighty to eighty-five candidates are interviewed each year, but only nine first-year residents are chosen. The program director, Dr. John Mullen, and the department chairman, Dr. Keith Lillemoe, meet with all the interviewees, which is more gracious than the previous structure.

When I was an intern applicant, house staff salaries were at a poverty level, which had just begun to be corrected by the impetus of the "heal in" at Boston City Hospital that doubled our first-year salaries. Thereafter, as salaries gradually increased, it became less advantageous for the hospital to use house staff for scut work that could be done by ancillary personnel. House staff, most of whom still have accrued enormous debt during their education, now have reasonable remuneration.

The two resident-run east and west services, founded in 1874, no longer exist and have been merged into the Churchill service, which is the trauma and acute care service. The chief resident position previously so sought after and usually filled by an individual who had already completed the requisite five years of general surgery residency, likewise no longer exists. All patients are now admitted under the name of an attending surgeon who is responsible for their care.

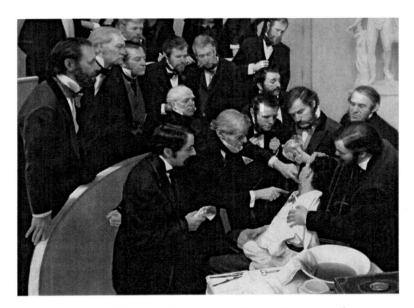

Painting in 2000 by Warren and Lucia Prosperi of a re-enactment of MGH's first use of ether anesthesia in 1846. Members of the MGH senior surgical staff participated. The resident staff posed a similar re-enactment in 1971. (Courtesy of the Massachusetts General Hospital)

The nature of diseases being treated on the surgical service as well as the specifics of their treatment have changed enormously. Part of this change in the spectrum of surgical disease is due to advances in treatment.

Minimally invasive and endovascular surgery now provide a good measure of the operative volume and have enhanced surgical care by several orders of magnitude. More and more procedures are done on an outpatient basis, and inpatient lengths of stay are more abbreviated. Advances in anesthesia and pain control have contributed to this improvement.

The rampant peptic ulcer disease in our patient population was previously treated operatively by gastrectomy and vagotomy. In patients with chronic peptic ulcer disease, the duodenum is heavily scarred down and contracted, making its closure technically difficult and prone to leakage. Many surgeons at this time made their reputation by their treatment of the "difficult duodenum," and several techniques for duodenal closure were associated with the names of the surgeons who popularized them—Lahey, Graham, Nissen, and Bsteh.

With the advent of effective drugs to treat gastric hyperacidity, operations for peptic ulcer disease are now rare. Today, the average candidate for the American Board of Surgery examination has only done one or two gastrectomies for ulcer disease, whereas a few decades ago, we did several dozen during our training.

One of our common tasks was iced saline lavage for upper gastrointestinal bleeding from esophageal varices or peptic ulcers. A house officer and a nurse would team up and have two large basins, one with iced saline, the other empty; two 50 cc syringes were filled with iced saline and irrigated down a nasogastric tube, the fluid aspirated back and emptied into the second basin. Hopefully, bleeding would stop at least temporarily, and operation could be planned electively if needed.

Since hernias are sometimes caused by increased abdominal pressure due to straining at stool in the presence of a colonic mass, part of the preoperative evaluation was an outpatient barium enema followed by a sigmoidoscopy performed after admission by the surgical intern. This relationship has long since been deemphasized because it is uncommon for a mass lesion of the colon to be causally associated with an inguinal hernia.

We kept patients hospitalized for six or seven days after routine operations because we did not trust them to go home with sutures in place. Half of a service with patients who did not need to be in the hospital prevented admissions for elective surgery. No longer.

Likewise, biliary tract disease and gallstones are evaluated and treated very differently. Prior to the advent of CT scanning and ultrasound, patients with suspected gallbladder disease underwent an oral cholecystogram (Graham-Cole test), swallowing up to a dozen pills, which would then opacify the gallbladder, allowing X-ray appraisal and identification of abnormalities. This test has long since been totally supplanted by ultrasound, which is simpler and quicker.

A frequent presentation at our mortality and morbidity conferences was a retained common bile duct stone after an open common duct exploration which accompanied a cholecystectomy (gallbladder removal). A retained stone can be a lethal problem if it obstructs the common bile duct, leading to cholangitis and Gram negative sepsis.

Repeat operations on the biliary tree can be technically difficult. Now, complicated biliary tract problems, such as common bile duct stones, are treated before operation by a skilled gastrointestinal endoscopist who can perform a procedure called a papillotomy, which opens the duodenal papilla to allow the stones to pass freely into the duodenum.

It was common before advanced imaging studies to admit people to the hospital with suspected appendicitis and then evaluate them with repeat physical examinations and white blood counts several times a day, usually performed by the house officer. The dictum was that if fifteen to twenty percent of appendectomies did not reveal a normal appendix, the surgeon was not being sufficiently aggressive in operating on acute appendicitis.

Now, the refinements of CT scanning have produced a quantum change in our approach to acute abdominal problems. Patients with abdominal pain and a negative CT scan can safely be sent home with the assurance that there is an extremely low risk of appendicitis, obviating the need for hospital admission and observation.

Varicose vein surgery is no longer a "tediometiculectomy," with the requirement to dissect innumerable veins below the fascia before ligating them. These procedures required a great deal of time to be done correctly. Incompetent saphenous veins can now be obliterated with catheter-based laser techniques, and if residual varicosities remain, they can be treated by phlebectomy or sclerotherapy, both outpatient procedures.

Likewise venous access techniques are unrecognizable from those performed several decades ago. We were often asked to perform "cut downs" for venous access in patients with no obvious veins for insertion of intravenous lines. The house officer needed to expose the vein under local anesthesia in the patient's bed with poor lighting and minimal if any assistance.

Unfortunately, the durability of this access was short-lived, and many patients had continuing access problems if prolonged intravenous therapy was needed. The development and refinement of catheter-based guidewire techniques has allowed intravenous lines to be inserted in major central veins under ultrasound guidance with a very high success rate, low morbidity, and long durability.

The increasing need for hemodialysis to treat chronic renal failure over the past several decades has necessitated construction of arteriovenous fistulas or grafts for hemodialysis. Now these procedures account for a significant portion of operative volume, and vascular surgeons have become more sophisticated in their construction.

Many previously common operations, such as a lumbar sympathectomy for arterial occlusive disease, staging laparotomies for Hodgkin's disease, and neck explorations for lymph node excision-cervicomediastinal exploration (CME) to identify extrapulmonary spread of lung cancer, are no longer performed.

Prior to advanced imaging techniques, the diagnosis of an intra-abdominal abscess was one of exclusion. If a patient had a persistent fever, a normal chest X-ray, no urinary tract infection, and a normal-appearing wound, he was presumed to have an intra-abdominal infection, and operation was reluctantly advised at a time when adhesions and inflammation made reexploration more hazardous. Today, most intra-abdominal abscesses or fluid collections can be drained with a small catheter inserted under CT scan guidance.

Perioperative antibiotic management has undergone considerable sophistication. We no longer give intravenous antibiotics for several days after operation because it is now understood that operative infections are caused by intraoperative contamination, and that a single dose of antibiotic given just prior to operation is superior treatment. Much of this research was done by Dr. John Burke at the MGH.

The success of split-thickness skin grafting depended on preventing fluid accumulation under the graft in the first twenty-four to forty-eight hours after operation , thus allowing it to become adherent to the recipient bed. Preventing fluid accumulation under the graft required the intern to "roll the graft" several times a day with cotton tip applicators to force the serum out. Toward the end of my residency, a mesh technique was developed which created a lattice pattern in the graft by passing it on a plastic backing through a roller, allowing it to be expanded to a predetermined ratio, so fluid could drain through the interstices, obviating the need for intern attention every few hours.

The emergency room, once the domain of the surgical service, is now run by an autonomous emergency department with its own residency program. Surgical residents are still physically present for surgical problems but share the necessary invasive procedures with the emergency room residents.

The previously punitive call schedule of being in the hospital every other night for most of five years has been replaced. Residents are now limited to an eighty-hour work week and must have time off after being on duty for twenty-four consecutive hours. On the private Baker service, most residents are on-call for six twelve-hour days. A separate house officer works as a "night float" from 6:00 p.m. to 6:00 a.m.

Physician extenders perform many of the important but boring tasks designated as scut that were so time-consuming for house staff: drawing bloods, starting intravenous lines, changing dressings, hanging blood transfusions, and dictating discharge summaries.

The Phillips House overlooking the Charles River has been physically replaced, but the entity still exists on the top three floors of the Ellison Building. The Baker Memorial Hospital, which was a self-contained building housing the semiprivate service, is no longer present. The Bullfinch Building is a national historic monument.

The free cafeteria meal for the house staff from 10:00 p.m. to midnight is now available from 9:00 p.m. to 10:00 p.m.—fewer and less hungry house staff on duty at night. It continues to provide an opportunity for on-duty residents to meet and discuss the day's events and to bond with their colleagues

The previous small cadre of visiting surgeons, all general surgeons, have been replaced with a much larger visiting surgical faculty. When Dr. Paul S. Russell became chairman several years before I arrived, he and the chair of anesthesia held the only named endowed chairs in the department. Several renowned surgeons had not been promoted above the level of associate professor because Dr. Edward D. "Pete" Churchill, Dr. Russell's predecessor, believed that one professor should be in charge. Currently, there are ten divisions within the Department of Surgery, fifteen Harvard Medical School professorships, and four endowed MGH chairs. Investigation has flourished, and total research expenditures in 2014 were $60 million.

*Four MGH surgery department chairmen. From
left to right: Drs.Paul S. Russell, Andrew L.
Warshaw, W. Gerald Austen, and Keith D. Lillemoe.
(Courtesy of the Department of Surgery)*

At weekly grand rounds, interesting and complicated cases were presented with an air of triumph by the residents, often with the patient standing mutely by. These rounds had a bit of the air of an elementary school show and tell, to which the patient's presence added little. This type of grand rounds has been largely supplanted by invited speakers.

Over the years, the teaching of surgery has changed, presumably permanently. Andy Warshaw told me that two major impediments to operative teaching have been the eighty-hour work week and the self-retaining retractor.

As house officers, we continually aspired to increase our competence and perform more complicated operations in each level of training. A well-motivated junior house officer would volunteer to replace the medical student as second assistant to observe and assist at an operation he hoped to be performing the following year. The eighty-hour work week has impeded this practice by limiting the number of hours residents may remain in the hospital. This prohibition is strictly enforced by credentialing bodies, and heavy fines are incurred if an institution deviates from it.

The development of fairly complex metallic retractors, like the Bookwalter or Omni, resembling erector sets and consisting of a fixed ring or frame with multiple interchangeable arms and retractor blades, has allowed major operations to be performed by one surgeon and one assistant, obviating the need for a second assistant.

Anesthesia and intensive care have improved. The respiratory ICU was begun in 1961 with five beds for patients on ventilators. Now the MGH has nine ICUs and 130 critical care beds.

Clinical research has changed. It was possible during my residency years to do retrospective clinical reviews based on the MGH experience. The chart notes were succinct and sequential, data was easily found, and the record room could easily find a large number of records, given a diagnosis code. The visiting staff was glad to help with planning and editorial advice.

Many of us developed areas of interest and expanded our knowledge base in this way. I wrote papers describing the MGH experience with perforated duodenal ulcers and with infected aortic aneurysms.

No longer. Even the charts for outpatient operations are thicker than those of forty years ago for complicated hospitalizations. HIPPA regulations impede access to patient charts to protect confidentiality, so that one needs "an honest broker" to access records which identify patients by name.

The breadth of general surgery has narrowed. Just as the Marine Corps preaches that "Every marine is a rifleman," Dr. Churchill believed that every surgeon was a general surgeon. But times needed to change. Dr. Austen wrote, "The MGH General Surgical Services, to my way of thinking, had tremendous strengths, but there were some deficits, too. I felt that we had to find a way to develop emerging specialties of surgery ... without jeopardizing the traditional strengths of general surgery."

Cardiothoracic surgery now requires a separate training program. Likewise, vascular surgery requires a two-year fellowship beyond general surgery training. A plastic surgery residency was established in the early 1970s so that general surgical residents do not have as extensive an experience in plastic surgery and burn management as they did several decades ago. Gynecology, previously our domain, allowed residents to become comfortable with operating deep in the pelvis, enhancing their comfort level with complex intestinal procedures and with self-identification as complete abdominal surgeons. Gynecology now has a separate department with its own residency program.

Several decades ago, residents finishing a five-year general surgery program felt comfortable performing any abdominal procedure, as well as most thoracic and vascular procedures and some plastic surgery procedures, such as skin grafts. Currently almost all residents at the Mass General and other training programs feel a need for additional training beyond general surgery residency. Whether this is occasioned by credentialing requirements to perform certain procedures or by a lack of confidence in their ability to be fully autonomous in the operating room is unclear. Over the past five years, all but two of the residents who finished the general surgery program have continued with a more advanced fellowship.

CHAPTER 12

Every major surgical training program has one or two particularly illustrious surgeons and usually an academically accomplished chairman. The MGH had an extraordinary depth of visiting surgeons who exercised leadership in the national surgical community and made major contributions to their specialties.

When Ashby Moncure, who was chief resident when I was an intern, gave his presidential address to the New England Surgical Society, he recalled his internship year and the group of nine visiting surgeons who were his teachers during his training, four of whom served as president of the American Surgical Association.

Between Ashby's internship and the completion of my own residency, this list of nine visiting surgeons had grown as the surgical staff expanded. Two of the visiting surgeons (Claude Welch and Jerry Austen) became presidents of the American College of Surgeons, as did Andy Warshaw, who was several years senior to me in the residency program and ultimately succeeded Jerry Austen as chief of surgery. Dr. Welch also served as president of multiple surgical societies. W. Hardy Hendren was one of the most skillful pediatric surgeons in the United States and established the subspecialty of pediatric urology. Paul S. Russell, department chairman when I began as an intern, made a number of major contributions to transplant immunology. Hermes C. Grillo was the father of tracheal reconstructive surgery and served as president of the American Association of Thoracic Surgeons, as did Mortimer J. Buckley, chief of cardiac surgery.

John Burke was a pioneer in burn therapy and surgical treatment of infections and helped develop the artificial skin. Jerry Austen became department chairman when I was a junior resident and exercised extraordinary leadership in the surgical community locally and nationally, launched cardiac surgery at the MGH, and was president of eight major societies.

The American College of Surgeons awards the Jacobson Award each year to a surgeon who has made innovative and crucial contributions to surgery. As of this writing, six of the twenty-one recipients of this award were MGH graduates, one of whom finished two or three years before I started; the remainder were either faculty members or residents with me during my training.

Joel Cooper received the award for lung transplantation and lung reduction surgery. Michael Harrison, chief of pediatric surgery at U.C. San Francisco, created the specialty of fetal surgery to correct developmental defects *in utero.* Judah Folkman made contributions to our understanding of tumor angiogenesis and was a potential Nobel laureate until his untimely death. John Burke and Hardy Hendren were recognized for their contributions to burn therapy and the development of techniques for reconstruction of complex urogenital abnormalities in infants, respectively. Jay Vacanti was honored for his work with tissue engineering.

During most of my training, the director of the training program was Dr. Leslie Ottinger. Les was a mentor and an example to all of us. He was comfortable doing complex abdominal, thoracic, and vascular procedures. His judgment and technical skills were peerless. Along with Ashby Moncure, Les was the go-to surgeon we called upon for advice with complex and difficult problems and when we or our family members needed surgical care.

Dr. Leslie W. Ottinger, director of the surgical residency (Courtesy of the Department of Surgery)

But what we appreciated most about Les was his unswerving, self-critical intellectual honesty and his dedication to patient care. When Les reached age 65, he decided to stop operating. Then he concluded that if he was no longer making hospital rounds and taking care of patients, he should not run the residency program, so Charles Ferguson succeeded him. The virtues that Les taught us have stood the test of time even though in today's medical world they are eroded by considerations of expediency and corporate economic goals. Les firmly believed that optimal postoperative care is provided not only by a surgeon, but by the patient's own surgeon.

Les addressed the MGH Surgical Society after an award was named for him and concluded with, "Although I doubt that any of you will have a fine career here as I did, I do wish that for you." We all wanted to be like Les when we finished training, but in a changing surgical world, it was not possible.

Why did everyone work so hard and perform at such a high level? I think the answer is that we all learn and teach by example rather than by dictum. The performance level among the house staff was so high that it propelled us to work harder.

Paul Russell wrote, "We revered the people we worked for. There were some marvelous people here with strong principles. They watched us pretty closely, and we wanted their approval. We wanted to be like them."

But the senior surgical staff, the visiting surgeons, were only half of our teachers. In large measure, the residents taught each other, woking side by side, often in the middle of the night. The quality of the teaching was exceptionally high.

We spent more time with each other than with our families. We respected each other and nurtured each other professionally. We had a common goal—to take exemplary care of our patients and become superior surgeons. When we talked about our careers decades later, we remembered patients we had cared for. We did not list the places we had worked, we just said, "I'm from the MGH."

The bond that developed among us, like the bond among soldiers or those who have borne hardships together, is permanent.

> We few, we happy few, we band of brothers.
> For he today that sheds his blood with me
> Shall be my brother. Be he ne'er so vile,
> This day shall gentle his condition.
> And gentlemen in England now abed
> Will think themselves accursed they were not here,
> And hold their manhoods cheap whiles any speaks
> Who fought with us on Saint Crispin's Day.
>
> —Shakespeare, *King Henry V*, Act IV, Scene iii

BIBLIOGRAPHY/ACKNOWLEDGEMENTS

A number of works were helpful in supplementing my recollections and augmenting my understanding of the rich history of the MGH.

The following historical works give an appreciation of the hospital's legacy:

Bull, W. and Martha Bull. *Something in the Ether: A Bicentennial History of Massachusetts General Hospital 1811–2011.* Beverly, MA: Memoirs Unlimited, 2011.

Castleman, Benjamin, ed. *The Massachusetts General Hospital 1955–1980.* Boston: Little Brown & Co., 1983.

Dretler, S.P., chairman. *Voices of the Massachusetts General Hospital 1952–2000: Wit, Wisdom and Untold Tales.* Brookline, MA: Lamprey & Lee, 2014.

Kitz., R.J., ed. *This Is No Humbug—Reminiscences of the Department of Anesthesia at the Massachusetts General Hospital 1969–1999.* Boston: Department of Anesthesia and Critical Care, Massachusetts General Hospital, 2002.

Washburn, F.A. *The Massachusetts General Hospital: Its Development 1900 to 1935.* Boston: Houghton Mifflin Co., 1939.

Additional writings provided insight into the evolution of the hospital, the surgical training program, and those who helped shape it:

Crichton, Michael. *Five Patients.* New York: Alfred A. Knopf, 1970.

Cutler B.S. "Robert R. Linton, MD: A Legacy of 'Doing it Right.'" *Journal of Vascular Surgery* 19 (1994): 95–103.

Grillo H.C. "Edward D. Churchill and the 'Rectangular' Surgical Residency." *Surgery* 136 (2004): 947–52.

Miller, G. Wayne. *The Work of Human Hands.* New York: Random House, 1993.

Moncure, A.C. "Tenax Propositi on Uncharted Seas." *Archives of Surgery* 136 (2001): 376–382.

Rutledge, R.H. "Good Cheers: Surgical Memoirs." *Archives of Surgery* 135 (2000): 1116–18.

Thomas, Lewis. *The Youngest Science—Notes of Medicine Watcher.* New York: The Viking Press, 1983.

Warshaw, A.L. "Department of Surgery, Massachusetts General Hospital, Boston." *Archives of Surgery* 138 (2003): 1173–74.

Welch, C.E. *A Twentieth-Century Surgeon: My Life in the Massachusetts General Hospital.* Boston: Massachusetts General Hospital, 1992.

The Massachusetts General Hospital Surgical Society Newsletter has contained informative communications from the alumni of the surgical residency over the years.

A number of colleagues and friends have been generous in sharing their recollections and experiences in the preparation of this book. My appreciation to George Andros, Edward Barksdale Jr., David C. Brewster, A. Benedict Cosimi, Willard (Bill) Daggett, Thomas F. Dodson, Matthias B. Donelan, Thomas K. Gutheil, Keith D. Lillemoe, Michael N. Margolies, James W. May, Ashby C. Moncure, John T. Mullen, John B. Mulliken, Thomas F. O'Donnell, Anthony S. Paton, W. Reid Pitts, Andrew Roberts, Paul S. Russell, Warren Sewall, Thoralf Sundt III, Robert Thurer, John Wesley, and William C. Wood.

Suzanne Williams, secretary to the chairman of the department of surgery, has been a help and source of encouragement throughout the preparation of this book.

Lightning Source UK Ltd.
Milton Keynes UK
UKOW02f0623171116

287833UK00001B/148/P